The Principles

Universal Enhancement

Praise for Tom Pomeranz and Universal Enhancement

Tom Pomeranz's wonderfully written volume could aptly be titled, 'Confessions of a Former Behaviorist.' With honesty, wit and reflection, he has traced his own journey as a practitioner and as an advocate.

In parallel, he traces the various service models (developmental, habilitation) that have led to a system where people with disabilities are 'fixed,' have problems and have limitations.

The author challenges the reader to *do with* rather than *for*, to focus on participation rather than readiness, and to believe in possibilities rather than limitations.

–Derrick Dufresne
Community Resource Associates

My family and I are segment hikers on the Appalachian Trail. I attended a training session led by Dr. Tom Pomeranz focusing on Universal Ehancement. Surprisingly, he used a term I had only seen associated with the Trail, the use of "stiles" to cross over barriers and move forward... precisely what occurs during a hike.

Dr. Pomeranz challenges us to offer support stiles to people with developmental disabilities. A stile is really a covenant of trust, a belief that it will afford safe passage.

The theories and maxims offered through Universal Enhancement foster personal achievement. They are methodologies, techniques to support people with developmental disabilities as they move along their life's path. Universal Enhancement provides ideas and is a compass that guides, even on those days when landmarks are few.

–Margaret J. (Peggy) Gould
The VISIONS Center

The Principles and Practices of
Universal Enhancement

Second Edition

by Thomas E. Pomeranz, Ed.D.

Edited by Virginia Vath
Foreword by Art Dykstra

High Tide Press
New Lenox, IL

Published by High Tide Press
2081 Calistoga Dr., New Lenox, IL 60451, USA
www.hightidepress.com

© 2001, 2009 Thomas E. Pomeranz, Ed.D.
All rights reserved. First edition 2001
Second edition 2009
Printed in the United States of America
01 09   1 2

Pomeranz, Thomas E. The principles and practices of universal enhancement, 2nd ed. / by Thomas E. Pomeranz, Ed.D.

ISBN 978-1-892696-41-0

Edits by Virginia Vath; designs by Diane J. Bell and Catrina J. Harris.

Second Edition
2009

To my wife, Diane–my partner, inspiration
and chief of the UE Police

Table of Contents

Foreword	xi
Preface	xiii
Acknowledgments	xvii
Introduction	xix

Section I: It Matters How We Say It

1. It Matters How We Say It: Using Universal Language	3
2. Two Visits and Some Observations	31
3. The Characteristics of the Institutional State of Mind	41

Section II: Challenging the Gatekeepers

4. Only Barrels Have Capacities	83
5. Gatekeepers and Other Exclusionists	97
6. Learning Through Participation	115

Section III: Obstacles to Opportunities

7. Supported Routines	139
8. Turning Obstacles into Opportunities	178
9. "Because We're Not Children Anymore"	187

Section IV: Venturing Beyond the Iron Gate

10. Beyond Mere Integration to Full Inclusion	207
11. The Elements of Getting a Life	227
12. Having a Life...and Beyond	259
About the Author	265

Foreword

In recent decades, a movement towards self-determination has brought about significant changes for persons with intellectual and developmental disabilities. Their choices about where and how and with whom to live and work and play have greatly expanded. For much of that time, Dr. Tom Pomeranz has been traveling the continent, teaching methods to help those who provide services and supports to accelerate these changes. His spirited jabs at the mindless, outdated methods people sometimes use to provide services and supports are alternately provocative and inspiring.

These past few years have seen the closing of many institutions in the United States and elsewhere in the world. Technology, medicine, psychology and information science continue to race forward and benefit persons who face challenges of daily living. But, those who provide services and supports cannot stop there. Their levels of adaptability, creativity and compassion must also move forward. Embracing change and innovation, asking the right questions, and keeping the focus on the person served will always drive exceptional quality in human service organizations.

The outcomes that we assist persons with disabilities to seek for themselves are becoming, more and more, a part of what the world recognizes as fair, appropriate and wise. However, the institutional state of mind that Dr. Pomeranz describes so well still exists in many places. So, even though some of the language in this book has changed to conform to current standards of professionalism, Dr. Pomeranz's message remains timeless.

Organizations across the United States and Canada have been guided by Dr. Pomeranz's compassionate and practical philosophies. And, they have adopted his strategies and techniques to bring about positive change. But, it is clear that many good people who have a say, or have a hand, in the lives of persons with disabilities have much to learn. The expectation is that you, and others in your organization who use this 2nd Edition of Universal Enhancement, will continue to learn and grow and enhance the lives of those you serve.

–Art Dykstra
Executive Director
Trinity Services, Inc.

Confessions of an Operant Intrusionist
A Personal Preface

Like many of my colleagues, I emerged from graduate school with a solid academic background in behavioral analysis. I had learned a great deal about the contingency management of behaviors. Upon graduation, I put all my knowledge to work, believing all my strategies were innovative as I put my abilities to the test in working with persons with intellectual disabilities.

Having spent a significant portion of my professional life training crisis teams to "control" outbursts of aggression; designing time-out rooms that met the technical requirements of state licensure and Medicaid standards; refining techniques for "take downs" and "basket holds"; and writing behavior "management" plans that used four staff persons to conduct an overcorrection procedure of two-hour duration, I now look back with a great deal of sadness and regret. I was doing what I was trained to do, doing what was state of the art at the time. I did not know better. In the "institutions" where I worked, I was surrounded by men and women engaged for endless hours in self-injurious behavior, lying on bare terrazzo floors in their own excrement.

I saw untold numbers of people injured by the aggressive behaviors of their peers, behaviors that were allowed to go unchecked for whatever reason. By doing something that would prevent self-injury, aggression and property damage, I had the opportunity to show that I cared for each of these individuals.

Like many others, what I failed to understand at that time was that my response to the inappropriate behaviors became, at the very least, a contributor to the maintenance of that very behavior. In some cases, my "intervention" may have been the primary cause. It was a vicious circle.

I was dealing with men and women who lived in stark and barren environments, persons who were denied even the basic opportunities for choice and decision-making. Neither I nor other staff ever asked them whom they would like to have assist them in their most private moments of being bathed or assisted with their toileting functions.

We did not seek to know what foods a person preferred. Rather, we as clinicians were satisfied that the food placed before the group met their nutritional requirements as assessed by the dietician.

The persons with whom they shared the ward or residence were "placed" there. We did not think to ask, "Would you like this person as your housemate?"

Schedules of reinforcement were designed and applied by behaviorists like myself to control those behaviors that we thought undesirable. Furniture was purchased, clothes provided, activities scheduled, and so on—all without the input and involvement of the person affected.

Many of the places in which I delivered my professional services had the air of displaced persons camps. No one seemed to be "at home." Everyone was in transit, awaiting an opportunity to move to a new place, a new home, a new life.

Looking back, it should have been obvious that a person residing in an environment that denies all opportunity for choice and control lives a life of *anomie*. This means: "If my life has no value, if my life has no meaning, I will behave in a way to cause your life not to have meaning or value either." The person living in anomie has "no name" and "no law," as the term indicates. He is not likely to care about me or my professional concerns, or even my futile attempts to show him that I am acting out of a sense of compassion and obligation.

Anomie is not, by any means, a phenomenon restricted to environments where persons with intellectual disabilities live. We saw anomie in Los Angeles, in the early summer of 1992. We saw a crowded community in which men and women felt they had no control over their lives, no power to make decisions that would influence their destiny. Those citizens, suffering the day-to-day life of urban anomie, behaved in ways to cause the lives of others to have no meaning or value—buildings were burned and looted, violence and rioting flared.

The men and women served in those big state facilities, as well as those who "moved up" to small, scattered site group homes, did not burn our buildings or rob us of our belongings. They did, however, demonstrate behaviors that caused the lives of the people around them to diminish in value. The anomie they suffered took its toll on everyone—a great toll.

I now think about all the effort expended in an attempt to control the behavior of others, when what was really needed was an opportunity—many opportunities—for those individuals to control their own destinies, to have a say-so, to have a life!

Ironically, the "treatment" caused the disease. The "therapeutic" environment—with its schedules, menus, assignments, programs, structure and anormalized rhythms—caused the very behaviors that I was so fervently trying to eliminate. In hospital parlance, "nosocomial infections" are those illnesses that are contracted in the hospital. A woman may enter the hospital for removal of her appendix and come out with a serious staph infection. The disease is caused by the treatment environment. Likewise, *nosocomial behaviors* emanate from the intended habilitative environment. Aggression, stereotypical behaviors, self-injury and property destruction are not symptomatic of an intellectual disability. These behaviors are a person's response to an insensitive and controlling environment—an attempt to communicate unmet needs, especially the need to have a say-so.

What then, as a behaviorist, is my response to all this? I spent several years developing a systematic approach that can be shared with others to support appropriate behaviors in persons we serve and support. The approach is called "Universal Enhancement." Simply stated, it says that people who have the opportunity to develop significant and valued relationships in their lives are more likely to increase their potential to have meaningful and valued lives. It says that people who have the opportunity to engage in preferred and meaningful activities with those valued others–choir, bike riding, work, walking, cooking, and so on–increase their opportunity to be free from anomie.

The goal of Universal Enhancement is to increase the opportunities to have valued relationships and personal belongings and the opportunity to make choices in one's life, thus precluding anomie and preventing the nosocomial behaviors I worked so hard to "manage" and "control." Even more exciting is the power of Universal Enhancement to help a person have a life. Expressions of anger are often communications of unmet needs. People want to have a life. As a result of my struggle with those I was attempting to "habilitate," I think I now understand.

The application of Universal Enhancement is not easy; it is a lifelong effort. It requires creativity and, most importantly, a belief that the men and women whom we support, regardless of their capabilities, can, with the provision of appropriate supports, participate as full members of our shared community. It is that participation that promotes the opportunity to develop meaningful relationships with others and enhances the lives of all people, regardless of IQ, disability, age, race, religion or status in life.

The words and ideas of a number of my colleagues appear in this book. In some Tales and other passages, language that may be considered inappropriate today has been left unchanged in order to maintain the integrity of that person's original writing. The basic messages contained in those sections remain timeless and significant.

–Thomas E. Pomeranz

Acknowledgments

As emphasized throughout this work, Universal Enhancement is not an invention, it is a discovery. My personal journey in this discovery was made possible with the support and guidance of numerous friends, colleagues and mentors. Their influence is reflected in the telling of the "tales" and the forming of the "maxims."

I am indebted to Vincent Pettinelli, who encouraged the writing of this book and taught me the importance of metaphors in teaching; Cleveland Corbett, who showed me how to build on people's strengths; Ray Anderson, who inspires administrative bureaucrats to remove barriers; and Mark Gold, Greg Monaco, Burton Blatt, Wolf Wolfensberger, Robert Perske and countless other teachers who inspired the vision of Universal Enhancement.

A special thanks to Virginia Vath, who provided her editorial skills coupled with a focused determination to get things done. Virginia's extensive support in polishing the book in preparation for publication is sincerely appreciated.

And, most importantly, my sincere gratitude to the thousands of people with intellectual disabilities who face the challenges of having a valued life, for giving me my passion.

Introduction

Universal Enhancement is not a new invention; it is, rather, a discovery. It is a key to unlock and open the closed doors that have served as barriers to countless persons who have been shut out of the world that most people take for granted. It is the key to a world in which all people are allowed to have a life, a magic key that requires not only using the right words, but also the motivation to do things differently. This book can be used as a key, but it is only a tool. You will have to bring your own resources to bear, as you use it to help people unlock new opportunities for themselves and their communities.

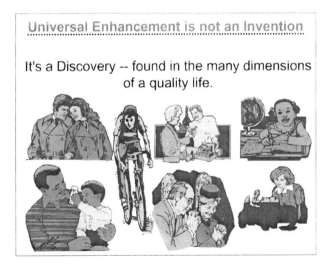

The notion that some people have been "cast out" from the mainstream of society will be used as the central metaphor. They are Outsiders. The primary examples of the phenomenon of being cast out are those persons who, because of diminished cognitive and adaptive abilities, are considered to have intellectual or developmental disabilities.

Universal Enhancement is "universal" because it applies equally to all conditions that have been used as the basis for excluding people from full participation in their own lives. The tools of Universal Enhancement are applicable to all of us, regardless of ability or disability, as we seek to "enhance" the quality of our lives. "Having a life" is a challenge we all face in some form. We all have our demons.

One reason intellectual disabilities is used as the primary exemplar is that the provision of services and supports for people with intellectual disabilities is the field in which I have had the most experience. Unfortunately, the other reason people with intellectual disabilities can serve as examples is that, for the most part, their lives have been stolen from them by the combined forces of ignorance, prejudice and fear.

Someone who works or lives with people who have mental illness, however, would see the opportunities of Universal Enhancement through the lens of that experience. The same holds true for people more familiar with the isolating effects of being elderly, having no parents or being an unwed mother. The principles hold true regardless of the exemplar. As you read through the book, you can mentally substitute the life circumstances with which you are most familiar or concerned (perhaps a challenge you personally experience) for the one used as an example.

The main narrative of this book can be read straight through. It provides all the history, principles and strategies you need for understanding Universal Enhancement. In it, you will find the following features.

Tales

Tales are illustrative stories, poems and collective conversation culled from the author's thirty-plus years of clinical and administrative experience. These stories demonstrate the principles of Universal

Enhancement and present concrete visions of how those principles change peoples' lives.

Toolboxes

Toolbox sections are practical techniques and procedures you can use as you implement the principles of Universal Enhancement. They will demonstrate innovative and effective ways of behaving. The checklist and program suggestions on Toolbox pages may be used in your work or efforts to assist others in enhancing the quality of their lives.

Maxims

Maxims are short, succinct phrases that encapsulate the tools and approaches of Universal Enhancement. They will form the core of this new approach, prompting and inspiring your new behavior. If your friends, neighbors and coworkers learn the Maxims, you will share a new vocabulary, a shorthand communication device we use to remind each other of what we are trying to do and where we are trying to go.

The author claims no exclusive rights to the ideas contained in this book because they are ideas found lying about in everyone's lives. They have been gathered and given form, but they came from everyone and thus belong to everyone. They are truly universal. It is my hope that, as you read what is compiled here, you will experience the same kind of "Aha!" feeling I have had as my new perceptions took shape. You might find yourself thinking, "These ideas are so simple; why didn't we think of and use them much earlier?"

The answer lies in our deeply rooted perception of people we see as being radically different from ourselves. This ability to see some groups of people as wholly "other" than ourselves has, historically, allowed us to act in ways we may later find incomprehensible. Upon touring the Holocaust Museum in Washington, D.C., a young man asked his father, "How could we have done these things to them?" And the father answered, "The first step was using the word 'them.' After that the rest was easy."

This book is the result of many thousands of hours spent working in the field of services for people with disabilities. I must express my deep appreciation to countless teachers, coworkers and friends, as well as to the people I have served and supported, who have helped shape the principles of Universal Enhancement. I hope this book will bring us all more such relationships, more opportunities to learn, and help us to exchange ideas and affect the lives of people.

1

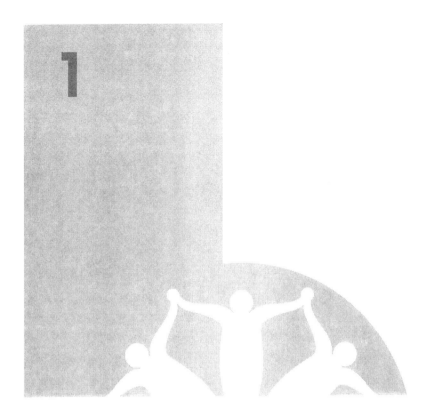

It Matters How We Say It

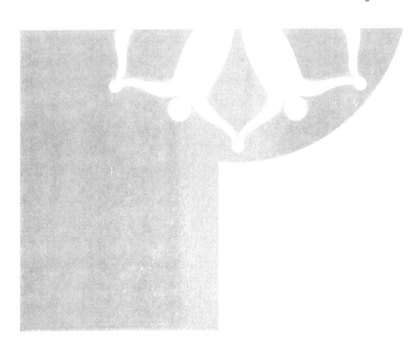

It Matters How We Say It: Using Universal Language

This book begins with a discussion of the ways we talk about people whose personal characteristics cause them to be treated as Outsiders. Making changes in our language is an important *first step* toward enhancing people's lives. But, this step is only one of the radical conceptual changes proposed with regard to our understanding of, and behavior toward, people who experience challenging life conditions and statuses. These *changes* and their ramifications accompany a paradigm shift that forms the centerpiece of our work.

Labeling

When nonspecific, categorical terms are applied to a person who has personal characteristics that are seen as setting him or her apart, it is called "labeling." A label purports to tell us what is inside the person, rather like labeling a can of tomatoes. The label on the can tells us what to expect when we open it–tart, red vegetables. We would be disappointed, maybe even upset, if we found something other than tomatoes in that can.

Unfortunately, labels applied to human beings often do not tell what is inside that person but what is missing. More often, they tell of defect or deficiency. Labeling a person "senile," "crippled," "homeless," "alcoholic," "crazy" or "retarded" indicates that some deficiency in physical ability, intellect or mental health will be found when we look inside.

One of the tragic consequences of these labels is that they often become self-fulfilling prophecies. We find just what the label told us we would find. The label alters our expectations, and this change in expectations limits our vision. Inside the person labeled "disabled" or "handicapped," we are not surprised to find inadequacies, defects and flaws. The label has directed attention away from the strengths, merits and uniqueness of that person.

> **MAXIM:** *We see things not as they are. We see things as we are. –The Talmud*

A good example of how labels affect how we treat people is the labeling that goes on in schools. A label applied to a child affects our expectations, and therefore the eventual outcome. In a famous experiment by Robert Rosenthal[1], labels about "academic potential" were given out, ostensibly as the result of accurate, predictive tests. In fact, the researchers had simply labeled a randomly selected twenty percent of each class as "potential spurters." These were children who were expected to show dramatic intellectual growth during the school year.

The teachers who worked with these children assumed the labels were accurate and expected them to do well. As a result, they did; forty-seven percent of the "special" children showed significant improvement in test scores (as opposed to nineteen percent of a control group). It is interesting to note that "ethical considerations" kept the experimenters from labeling a group of children "slow" or "retarded" in order to see if their academic development declined because of the label.

Labeling has an historical context. The labels applied to people change with time and accepted custom just like any other use of language. Consider, for example, the search for terminology that transcends racial stereotypes—"coloreds," "Negroes," "blacks," "persons of color" and "African-Americans." Scholars have written many monographs on the social and intellectual currents that helped to determine

---

[1] Rosenthal, R., and Jacobson, L. *Pygmalion in the classroom: Teacher expectation and pupils' intellectual development.* New York: Rinehart and Winston, 1968.

which terms were in vogue at particular times in our nation's history. A glance at the painful lessons highlighted by this kind of linguistic history is the best answer to those critics who say, "They're only words. What difference does it make what we call people?"

We are used to the notion that the epithets applied to people because of their racial, ethnic or religious affiliation have the capacity to wound, and that words can demean and degrade a person. As children, most of us were taught not to use offensive words for racial or ethnic groups. And today, if we were to use such terms in public, chances are someone would challenge our ignorance.

Yet, you may have given little thought to the words you use to describe people whose personal attributes have caused them to be set apart. Because no one challenged you to think about them, you may have used the terms "crippled," "retarded" or "crazy" without considering the impact this has on your behavior or on the people you reference.

Unfortunately, disparaging words that refer to one's handicap are often still accepted in a society that has learned not to tolerate racial or ethnic slurs. Too frequently, people with conditions that prevent them from advocating strongly for themselves become the targets of labels that wound like darts.

The reason labels can be so harmful is that they serve as indicators of how the person using them is thinking or feeling. When receiving communication from another person, we assume a relationship between the language used and the attitudes held. For instance, a person who makes demeaning comments about women may not be seen as doing actual harm with those words. But, the words indicate the presence of attitudes that can be harmful in a way the words themselves are not. This is true because negative attitudes drive behavior, and where the attitude is tolerated, there is little chance the behavior will be censured.

Throughout this book, the terms *Revered*, *Us* and *Outsiders* are used to show the distinctions made between people who are deemed worthy of dignity, respect and opportunity, and those who are not. I use these labels with full awareness of the irony of doing so. The term Outsiders captures the experience of persons who have been relegated to inferior status by Us because of their unique personal characteristics or attributes.

We must become aware that the use of labels says more about our fears and prejudices than it says about the person to whom the label is applied. No one asks to be an Outsider; they are cast into the role.

Disability Labels

The labels applied to people who have disabilities or other limiting conditions almost always carry pejorative connotations. Such terms point out what is lacking in the person. The current trend, based upon an increased emphasis on dignity and respect, is to use the term "intellectual disabilities" instead of "mental retardation." The field has acknowledged the overriding negative connotation associated with the term mental retardation.

Over the years, the terms applied to persons with intellectual disabilities have undergone many changes, just as the approaches to their participation and presence in society have. In the 1920s, it was acceptable professional practice to refer to persons with intellectual disabilities as "morons," "idiots" and "mental defectives." These legal/

medical classifications sometimes served as an honest attempt to look at the specific and varying needs of persons who had different degrees of disability. But, more often, they served to distance the "regular" or "normal" people from those who were seen as not quite human.

The labels focused on needs, limitations and deficiencies rather than on characteristics that were unique and special about a particular human being. Indeed, the labels often made us see and, unfortunately, treat the person as though he or she were on the other side of an unbridgeable gap between Us and Them. Someone referred to as a "moron" was frequently seen and treated as a member of a different caste or species. It is hardly possible to perceive and understand a moron as sharing in the same sorts of abilities, hopes and dreams that we see in our friends and neighbors.

Labels can serve to distinguish one group from another–the "sheep" from the "goats" or the "wheat" from the "chaff." Usually, however, it is only the less valued group that gets labeled. Consider the difference between being considered a person of "profound intellect" and a person who is "profoundly retarded."

If we call a person who has a condition that makes him different from most people a "defective," are we willing to also label the other side of the division, the rest of the people (Us) as "normatives"? Would we say of the person who is walking to the office in a neatly pressed business suit, "Look at that normative?" Not likely. A person who is valued, respected and seen as a complex and multifaceted human being is generally not labeled like a can of tomatoes.

For instance, we do not usually label our friends, coworkers or relatives–people we consider to be our equals. We might say of a friend, "John is really smart; he knows so much" or "Loretta is having trouble with that new job. Sometimes she just doesn't seem to get it." If John and Loretta are friends (or family members), we are not likely to use the technical jargon of psychology, describing John as "high-functioning" or Loretta as "deficient." Those are terms we reserve for people who are "Other than Us." When referring to people we respect and esteem, we use language that reflects our sense that they are our equals.

Using a term like "high functioning," on the other hand, proclaims that though the person referred to may have recognizable abilities, he or she really is not our equal.

We all appreciate the fact that people vary with respect to their competence, aptitude or talent. Each of us is a unique blend of abilities and disabilities. When we proclaim, "Larry can fix any kind of machine" or "Susie has a real talent for music," we are saying something particular about each person's behavior, something we know they do well. Even if we were to say something about a lack of ability, such as, "Larry *has* no mechanical aptitude" or "Susie *has* a tin ear," we are still describing an attribute of that unique person's behavior.

When we say, "Michael *is* mentally retarded" or "Harriet *is* a cripple," we do not reveal anything about who the person is, even though our language appears to do so. Indeed, we are denying that person's individuality by relegating him or her to a category with a label. By proclaiming that Michael is mentally retarded and Harriet is a cripple, we are free to see both of them as part of an undifferentiated mass we know as "the handicapped"–people tarnished and likely to be treated as Outsiders.

MAXIM: *People with intellectual disabilities are not broken; they do not need to be fixed.*

Thinking we know something about Michael and Harriet allows us to be complacent. We feel no need to do the things necessary to get to know them better. We are not likely to behave in the ways we usually do toward people with whom we would like to have a relationship. For their part, Michael and Harriet are likely to respond in kind.

Labels filter our observations, often directing us toward what is most lacking in a person–their needs and/or deficiencies rather than their strengths and gifts. It is, therefore, instructive to see how our conceptual eyes are opened when we focus on changing our language to enhance the way we talk about people and their circumstances.

For example, when we stop referring to "the Laurel Street Group Home" and instead talk about "the house at 51 Laurel Street," the ownership shifts. The house now belongs to the people who live there, rather than to the people who work there.

Simply changing our verbiage from "He's a head banger" to "Sometimes he hits his head against the wall when he's upset" shifts the perspective. We no longer see the behavior as representative of the person's essential nature but shift to an understanding of the behavior as just part of a whole, one element in a person's repertoire of relating to his or her world.

Referring to Gail, a thirty-five-year-old woman who lives in the group home, as "the person who is cooking dinner tonight" and to Harold, who works there, as "her support" keeps us from devaluing Gail's efforts. It prevents us from taking away her rightful choices and seeing her as a child by thinking, "Oh, isn't she a good little helper."

Regardless of whether they are positive or negative in impact, labels are always prejudicial. They are barriers to spending the time and attention we need to get to know individual human beings.

The Offending Pronoun

When we refer to "Michael, the retarded person," and "Harriet, the cripple," we think we know something about each person because we know something about Them. "Them" is the offending pronoun here, as in, "you know how *they* are." It allows us to categorize and dismiss whole groups of people as if their common traits were more important than the uniqueness of each individual.

When the group referred to is one that is generally demeaned, even a professional, descriptive term can take on the connotation of epithet and slur. Take, for example, the terms "spastic" and "cripple." These words have definite denotations, the standard definitions you would find in a dictionary. "Spastic" means "of, pertaining to, or characterized by spasms." In Britain, particularly, the term is used to refer to people who have cerebral palsy. "Cripple" means "one who is partially disabled or lame." The definition is simply a description of a condition.

But when we use these terms as epithets, they devalue, demean and disparage. When someone falls down or drops something, the cruel observer comments, "What a spaz!" When a young woman has to use crutches following a skiing accident, her friends laugh and jokingly call her "Crip." When a descriptive term is designed to denote what is missing from a person's repertoire of abilities, it quickly takes on a negative connotation of difference, disability and disparagement.

"They" attracts connotations like a magnet. We are all too familiar with the use of "they"–the offending pronoun–to devalue racial or ethnic groups, as in "They have a good sense of rhythm" or "They're only interested in money." The use of They allows people to be seen not as individuals but as stereotypes. A stereotype, "an oversimplified conception, opinion, or belief" (*The American Heritage Dictionary*), makes us think we know something about a person or group before we have any specific experience of them.

Thus, we may think we know that "the retarded" are childlike, oversexed, unable to make choices, really cute and lovable, odd smelling, child molesters, or a host of other stereotypical characteristics. We may think we know that "the blind" have "a sixth sense" or increased musical ability. Or, we may believe we know that "the elderly" like to play cards or live only in the past.

What happened to Michael and Harriet?

People First

What happened is that we forgot that Michael and Harriet, like our friends and associates, are people first. Michael is a person (first) with (the characteristics of) an intellectual disability (second)–"a person with intellectual disabilities." That does not really tell you much about him, and if you are not careful in your thinking, the single fact of Michael's disability may distract you from other things about Michael that are much more significant. Michael is also friendly and outgoing, has a great sense of humor, and has difficulty walking due to some paralysis in his right leg. He is a person with unique characteristics of his own, among which is the fact that he scored twenty-eight on a recent test of intelligence (IQ) and could not sing the words when his friends sang "Happy Birthday" to him when he turned forty.

If we refer to someone as "a person with a hearing impairment" or "a person with cerebral palsy," we see the person first and the challenge they live with second. It thus becomes more likely that the "difference" will be seen as just one characteristic of that person, not his or her essential nature. If I wear glasses, that does not make me "a myope." Myopia (nearsightedness) is not what I'm all about; it is just one of the untold number of aspects that make up the complex and multifaceted person I am.

It matters how we talk about people–it matters a lot. The words we use reflect how we think and how we value (or devalue) the focus of our language. The words we use when talking about people are a good predictor of how we are likely to act toward and with them. If we see Harriet as a person first, we can leave our stereotypes behind and develop a real relationship with a real human being. We can allow ourselves to be open to Harriet, rather than hamstringing ourselves with prejudices and prejudgments, which too often turn into self-fulfilling prophecies.

Of course, you may never have thought about the language you use. You may have learned to use labels unconsciously and innocently from those around you, without considering their impact. The tools in this book offer a different way of speaking, a different way of doing things to promote "talking the talk" as you begin to "walk the walk" toward Universal Enhancement.

Universal Language

One way to demonstrate a changed mind is to demonstrate changed speech. Using Universal Language, a language that can be applied to everyone, is a first step.

The rule for Universal Language is simple: Use the words appropriate for talking about and with your family and friends, and the words they use when talking about and with you. If you have any friends you refer to as "high functioning," then you could comfortably use that

> **UNIVERSAL LANGUAGE**
>
> *The words and language I use when talking about my friends, the words and language my friends use when talking about me is Universal Language.*
>
> When are you moving out of your apartment and moving into your new home?

term when referring to people with intellectual disabilities. Chances are good, however, that you would more likely refer to your friend as "capable," "competent" or just "smart."

People who work in the business of providing services and supports to people who have been cast Outside are particularly guilty of the kind of jargonizing language that sets people apart rather than bringing them together. We set people apart by using language that suggests we are in control of their lives. We may find ourselves saying people are "admitted" to or "discharged" from "our" group homes. On the other hand, we say that we "moved in" to our new homes and will "move out" when we decide to live somewhere else. When referring to Outsiders, we say that someone who does not like being told what to do is "noncompliant"–meaning she does not comply with our demands. But, the term we use with a recalcitrant spouse is more likely to be "uncooperative" or "stubborn."

We often refer to someone who cannot walk as a "non-am." In fact, a host of stereotypical terms are used frequently by people who provide services to Outsiders who engage in inappropriate behavior–"head banger," "runner," "floor sprawler," "rectal digger," "smearer," and on and on. If you do not work with people who are disenfranchised, you may not be familiar with the variety of terms that are used as clinical colloquialisms to describe a particular group of people. It is not the kind of language we use with our family and friends. If you are currently working with a specific Outside population, you may want to become more sensitive to the many shorthand references used in your field to characterize the less desirable attributes of those you serve.

The rule for Universal Language is easy to follow. Before using a term, just ask yourself whether or not this is something you generally use to describe the people in your life. A specialized term that is reserved for use only toward a person who is seen as different is a term that differentiates Us from Outsiders.

What to Call "Them"

In recent years, there has been extensive debate among professionals in various fields about what to call the people they serve and support. How can we differentiate those who provide services from those who receive them? What should we call "those people"?

At the turn of the 20th Century, in the state-operated schools and hospitals, the standard term for a person living there was, not surprisingly, "patient." Later, those facilities were viewed more as homes than hospitals, so the preferred term became "resident." When the model evolved toward the provision of necessary services, the recipients of those services were known as "clients." In the private sector, we sometimes call the people who use our services "consumers" or even "customers."

But, you must remember that when we label those we serve, we label ourselves, as well. When they were "patients," we were "therapists." When they were "clients," we were "habilitators." When they were "consumers," we were "providers." Each change in labeling reflects a change in the paradigm, the governing set of philosophies and ideas that drives our service delivery system. The current vogue of the use of "consumers," for instance, reflects our concern with the funding of services, distinguishing those who purchase services from those who vend them.

MAXIM: *Universal Language is the words and language I use when talking about my friends and family and the words and language they use when talking about me.*

When a person is participating fully in his or her life, one label is not enough to describe the roles he or she fills. We are all "residents" of the place where we live. We are "patients" when we go to the doctor. We are "clients" of our attorney or accountant. And, we are "consumers" when we purchase a new refrigerator. Each label requires a different set of behaviors, skills and competencies. Since we "normatives" are seen as being able to occupy a wide range of roles, we are seldom limited by any of the labels applied to Us. In fact, we hold many of these roles simultaneously, moving in and out of them with ease–and without permission.

Arguing about what is the most acceptable thing to call Them misses the point. By seeking an all-purpose label, we demonstrate that we are still thinking about people in categories rather than as individuals. We are looking for some shorthand way our language can indicate the difference between Us and Them without being derogatory or casting a negative connotation. But, we are still emphasizing the castaway status of those we label.

Any label that does not carry the connotation of Us is one that indicates the presence of aliens, people who need to be treated differently from our loved ones and associates. Universal Language seeks to do away with labels entirely by speaking only of individuals and their unique attributes. What had been labels can become temporary descriptors only, telling us something of the relationship between two people. People will be seen as patients by their doctors, as residents by their neighbors, as consumers by the store clerk, and as clients by their case manager or attorney.

MAXIM: *It's not what people have; it's what they do not have.* ™

As the following Tale illustrates, the problem lies in whatever supports or services or rights the person with a disability *does not have*, not whatever unique characteristics she *does have*.

TALE

You and I
by Elaine Popovich
Lutheran School Services, Midland, Missouri

I am a resident. You reside.

I am admitted. You move in.

I have behavior problems. You are rude.

I am noncompliant. You don't like being told what to do.

When I ask you out to dinner, it is an outing. When you ask someone out, it is a date.

I don't know how many people have read the progress notes people write about me. I don't even know what's in there. You didn't speak to your best friend for a month after she read your journal.

I make mistakes during my check-writing program, and some day I might get a bank account. You forget to record some withdrawals from your account. The bank calls to remind you.

I wanted to talk with the nice-looking person behind us at the grocery store. I was told that it was inappropriate to talk to strangers. You met your spouse in the produce department when he was shopping and couldn't find the bean sprouts.

I celebrated my birthday yesterday with five other residents and two staff members. I hope my family sends a card. Your family threw you a surprise party. Your brother couldn't make it from out of state. It sounded wonderful.

My case manager sends a report every month to my guardian. It says everything I did wrong and some things I did right. You are still mad at your sister for calling your mom after you got a speeding ticket.

I am on a special diet because I am five pounds over my ideal body weight. Your doctor gave up telling you.

I am learning household skills. You hate housework.

I am learning leisure skills. Your shirt says you are a "couch potato."

After I do my budget program tonight, I might get to go to McDonald's if I have enough money. You were glad the new French restaurant took your charge card.

My case manager, psychologist, RN, occupational therapist, physical therapist, nutritionist and house staff set goals for me for next year. You haven't decided what you want out of life.

Some day, I will be discharged...maybe. You will move onward and upward.

The Competency-Deviancy Hypothesis

The issue of language that excludes others leads us to a consideration of the basis for the exclusion. The person's perceived degree of competence is one factor that plays a prime role in deciding who is eligible to be Inside and who will be cast Outside. This perceived competence level leads us to acceptance or alienation, to comfort or threat.

Our society places a high premium on competence and the absence of defect. We in Western developed nations especially encourage competition, which, we say, motivates people to do their best. Those persons with the most marketable skills, whether it be forcefully arguing in court, artfully patching up an ailing heart, or consistently throwing a round ball through a hoop, are considered the most valued. Typically, people with competitive skills and abilities make the money and receive the acclaim of our competitive culture. They are revered.

Competency-Deviancy Hypothesis

The more competent you are, the more deviant a society will allow you to be without devaluing you.

Not only is money and fame typically extended to people with competence, but also tolerance and acceptance of difference. We tolerate a wide range of flamboyant, idiosyncratic and, some might say, *deviant* behavior from people recognized as competent. If they want to wear outrageous clothes, espouse odd political views or even treat coworkers rudely, people are not likely to reject them. People commonly tolerate the wealthy and famous person showing up half an hour late to the meeting. When Howard Hughes refused to shake people's hands because he thought everyone was contagious, he was seen as "eccentric," not as an Outcast.

What we see operating here is the Competency-Deviancy Hypothesis. Basically stated, it says: "The more competent you are, the more deviant society will allow you to be without devaluing you."

MAXIM: *The more competent you are, the more deviant society will allow you to be without devaluing you.*

If I am a distinguished professor on my way to a lecture, waiting coolly at a bus stop, reading my economically folded *Wall Street Journal* and glancing occasionally at my Rolex watch, it is not likely that those in my presence will comment about my unkempt hair or the Mickey Mouse T-shirt I am wearing under my suit jacket. I am obviously competent; therefore, I am less likely to be devalued.

On the other hand, if I am mumbling to myself and shuffling along with an awkward gait because I am in the later stages of Alzheimer's disease, and if I gaze aimlessly around the bus stop, trying to recall my destination, then onlookers will assume that I have limited competence. They will offer me little, if any, latitude in their judgment of my appearance or my behavior. They will likely see my Mickey Mouse T-shirt as a validation that people like me are indeed childlike. This is true even if I used to be just as competent as the professor who now wears the same shirt. People may see my unkempt hair as an indication that whoever cares for me is not doing an adequate job, perhaps suggesting that I am not worthy of such care.

They may assume that since I cannot care for myself and no one else cares for me, they do not care about me, either. They may then feel completely justified in saying to me, in a tone of voice usually used with a four-year-old, "How are you today? Did they forget to comb your hair this morning? Here, let me straighten it up for you." If they then reach out to adjust my hair for me, they have lost any chance of seeing me as a retired businessman, age eighty-two, on his way to see his buddies at the senior citizens center. They will fail to see a man who is valued by his friends and loved by his family. These unthinking people devalue me and my efforts at overcoming my condition. They see me as someone not worthy of the respect usually afforded strangers and passersby, and put me in the group labeled They.

Three Groups: Revered, Us and Outsiders

Having established the importance of the principles of Universal Language and explored the mechanisms by which people are judged in the Competency-Deviancy Hypothesis, we can now put forth a model of the workings of Exclusion and Inclusion.

The circles in the "Courtesy" figures on pages 19 and 20 depict three groups of people. In the first circle, labeled *The Revered*, are people such as Albert Einstein, Mother Teresa, Madonna, Thomas Edison,

Leonard Bernstein, Martin Luther King, Jr., Thomas Jefferson, Marie Curie, Stephen Hawking, Leontyne Price–brilliant, famous people. You could add your own choice of names to this group. It is competence that binds these people together in one company. We are always seeking people for inclusion in this group because they represent the competence we all revere.

In the second circle, labeled *Us*, are you and me, just ordinary, everyday people–Normatives. We are people who have not achieved prominence as the result of any particularly significant accomplishment. We live our lives in an ordinary, decent manner, engaging in the activities that are expected of good citizens. We have only demonstrated everyday, run-of-the-mill competence, but others in our communities generally accept us.

In the third circle, labeled *Outsiders*, are people who failed one or more elements in a battery of required tests. These tests are not a special kind of scrutiny applied only to a select group. We all had to pass them; they are among the rites of passage into *acceptance*. In order to be in the accepted groups, society requires all of us to be able to walk up and down a flight of stairs unassisted, or state our name and age when asked. If you are unable to do these things that "normal" people (those in the majority) do, or meet the standards

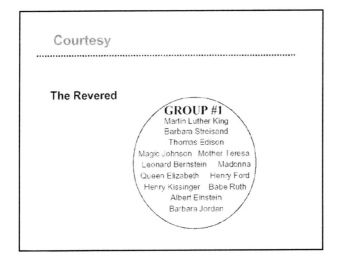

that we have established in order to be in with Us, you are cast into Group 3–the Outsiders.

Since competence is so revered in our culture, it should come as no surprise that people who fail certain tests are almost always assigned to Group 3. The test they failed could have been one that measures a person's ability to read an arbitrary line on the Snellen eye chart. Failures of this test become "the blind." Or, they may have failed the test that determines whether one can hear a sound at a

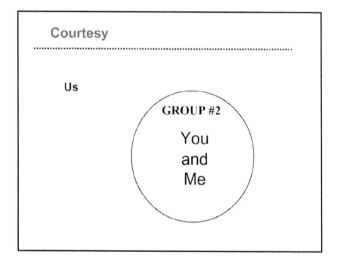

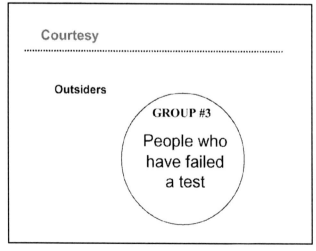

particular decibel level. These failures are labeled "the deaf," so they can be grouped with others of "their kind." Some failed the walking test, owing to their inability to walk up and down a flight of steps unassisted. They are "the crippled." (It does not matter if you call them "the physically challenged"–the label still puts them in the group with the incompetents.)

Some have failed the "ideal body weight" test and become "the obese." Others have no permanent address, no place to lay their head or keep their belongings. These are "the homeless." A small, but not insignificant, group failed the IQ test, which is to say they came up with scores lower than seventy. These belong with "the intellectually disabled." And, all are Outsiders.

Courtesy and Respect: The Ties That Bind

What difference does it make to which group you are assigned? The most important difference is the way we behave toward people in each group. Though the Revered are indeed deviant or different from the "norm" in important ways, the differences are *valued*. In meeting anyone elevated to the status of being Revered, you might be a little in awe. You might refer to him or her as "Sir" or "Ma'am." It would make little or no difference to you that Einstein was wearing two different

---

Factors Influencing Courtesy

The more radical your clothing and hair style
The more pronounced your foreign accent
The more orthodox your religious beliefs
The darker your skin
The more extreme your cultural practices
OR
The more disabled you are...

The more likely it is that courtesy will be withheld.

colored socks or forgot to comb his hair. It would not matter that Thomas Jefferson owned slaves and possibly fathered a child by one of them. You would learn to be patient with Professor Hawking's need to compose his replies on a speech synthesizer. You would likely treat these people with deference and respect. Their impressive competence tends to allay any misgivings you might have about their idiosyncrasies.

The people in Group 2 also receive our respect, or at least what we think of as common courtesy. Indeed the word "courtesy" has its roots in the "court" of kings and queens, the place where the ultimate Insiders practiced the form of manners and respect that showed they were well bred and worthy of consideration.

Courtesy is a demonstration of awareness of equality. If we do not extend courtesy to a particular person, such failure implies that we do not hold that person in a position of equality. We say "please" and "thank you" to people we respect, our equals. We are sensitive enough not to call attention to a colleague's bizarre appearance in public. He is one of Us. Nor would we stare at the lady in the grocery store who wears a bouffant hairdo, streaked pink in the middle. She is quiet, smells good, and says "Hi" as she decides on which wine to serve with the pasta shells. She, too, is one of Us. We do not interrupt when two people are talking with each other, or listen in on someone's apparently private conversation. We send each other "Get Well," "Happy Birthday" and "I'm sorry I hurt your feelings" cards. We are all competent, "regular" people, and are therefore entitled to–and worthy of–respect, decency and courtesy.

But, what about the people in Group 3? What about the "failures," those whose deficiencies call out as loudly as Mother Teresa's abilities? How do we treat Them?

The main thing that distinguishes people in Group 3 is that, although their separation often entitles them to supports and services not accorded to the other groups, they are seldom the recipients of the same kind of courtesy and respect. What is demanded, expected, and even taken for granted by those of us who have "earned" inclusion in Groups 1 or 2 is unavailable to them. Being Outsiders, the people in

Universal Enhancement Moments

- Referencing the person in respectful language
- Sharing a smile and a sense of humor
- Advocating for the person's rights
- Making introductions to promote relationships
- Listening to understand what is being communicated
- Being patient
- Having fun together
- Asking permission prior to assisting in moving or transferring
- Providing eye contact when conversing
- Knocking on a bedroom or bathroom door before entering
- Encouraging and supporting participation in all daily routines
- Speaking softly
- Using an age-appropriate tone of voice
- Offering options to support self-determination
- Celebrating even the smallest of accomplishments

Moments captured, not on video, but in the heart

Group 3 can be treated as aliens or foreigners who are unworthy of respect. They are not our equals.

Outsiders are individuals; they differ from person to person just as much as individuals in groups 1 and 2. But Outsiders, as persons, often lose focus in our minds. They blur into a hazy image made of one part cute poster child, one part half-forgotten experiences, more than a little fear, and a large dose of basic, stereotypical prejudice. We label people in Group 3 with the offending pronoun *They*. Once we see Them instead of individuals, we are free to act on our prejudicial judgment.

We can declare that we really would not like Them to move into our neighborhood ("property values, you know"). We are unlikely to say such a thing about people like Us being shown around by the realtor.

TOOLBOX
Using the Tools of Courtesy

We may not think of courtesy as a "tool" that helps others get a life. However, it demonstrates respect, consideration and a sense of equality–important elements of Inclusion in community life.

◆ When addressing anyone, say "Please," "Excuse me," "Thank you" and "May I?"

> MAXIM: *Do not speak any louder than necessary for the person to whom you are speaking to hear you.*

◆ Encourage people to use their abilities to support others who have disabilities.
  - A person who cannot speak can assist one who cannot walk.
  - A person who knows how to write can help someone who cannot to write and sign a bereavement card for a coworker whose father died, or a Thank You note for a gift received.

◆ Demonstrate appropriate greetings when you meet someone. Shake hands, make eye contact and say, "Hello."

◆ Introduce people as people. For example, "This is my friend Cindy" rather than "This is Cindy. She's one of our clients."

◆ Encourage opportunities to answer the phone or the doorbell. These are opportunities to practice courtesy skills.

◆ Give prompts as needed. For example, it is appropriate to say, "We need to keep our voices down in here because other people are reading."

- Use eye contact. The mind gives an emotional hug through eye contact. It says, "I value you. I am listening."
- Respect privacy. Privacy is a demonstration of courtesy.
- Do not interrupt the conversations of others.
- Ask people if they would like to be helped. Do not impose help. Such imposition is often perceived as condescending.
- Treat everyone with the same courtesy you would like for yourself. For example, most of us prefer empathy ("I understand") to sympathy ("Oh, you poor thing").
- Corrective feedback should always be given quietly. It only concerns the person with whom you are sharing the feedback.

We can get up and leave the area when a group of Them comes in, covering our fear with an uncertain smile. We may avert our eyes, cross to the other side of the street, or gather our children to us like a hen that sees a hawk. We may keep our distance, a distance that arises from the unexpressed fear that closer association with these Outcasts will jeopardize our cherished Normative status.

Sometimes, we justify our avoidance of Outsiders by our "understanding" that They do not really know what is happening. We may believe that They do not possess the same kinds of feelings to be hurt or sensitivities to be trampled on as we do. They are not part of the web of social relationships we call community.

Most of us know that it is wrong to stereotype people who are different, strange or less capable than ourselves. Our mothers told us not to stare. We walked five miles in the walk-a-thon for the "crippled children." We wore "Blue Jeans for Babies" as a fund-raiser. We are right thinking, caring people, so our exclusion of Outsiders from courtesy and respect must have some acceptable justification.

One of the ways our prejudice toward Outsiders is justified is our observation that They often do not demonstrate courtesy toward us.

People with intellectual disabilities or mental illness, who have lived for long years in institutional settings lacking in everyday decency, are sometimes rude and awkward in their social approaches. They may not bathe regularly, and may stare or point. Their eyes may not meet ours when we try to talk with them. Since they do not treat us with courtesy, we can justify our discourtesy. That is why it is so important for those of us who work with people who "act different" (regardless of the cause of the difference) to be role models of courtesy.

We must demonstrate how to treat people with respect—as equals—because people who are seen as having "bad manners" are automatically looked down on as being somehow inferior, as being Outsiders.

Sometimes, though, because we know exclusion is wrong, we may go to the opposite extreme. We may patronize people who have been cast as Outsiders and treat them with elaborate sham respect. We want to open doors, pick up fallen items, speak for them—generally "help out" and "do for." But by doing that, we may also establish the boundary line between the Outsiders and Us, building fences between the Groups.

Nothing points this up more clearly than when the person who uses a wheelchair says, "Don't push me. I can do it myself." When we force "help" onto another person, we devalue his or her abilities. We assume the person is less able than we are and therefore needs help. We place ourselves firmly in Group 2, closer to the rich and famous and farther from those we see as poor and helpless.

Cast Aside

It is important to understand that the relegation to Outsider status is not a consequence of simply being different. It is, rather, a result of being different in a way that is not valued, that is demeaned. Because we devalue the differences shown by Outsiders, we may tend to behave toward them in ways that diminish the quality of their lives. We may deprive them of rights and opportunities, and put them in a distinct group from which the only hope of escape is the passing of an impossible test designed by the Insiders.

The people who have been placed in the Outsider group did not ask to be there. Most Outsiders achieved that status through some accident of fate over which they had no control. They are there simply because they do not fit what the majority of society has decided is the correct and acceptable way to be.

And even if a person's condition is the result of some "fault" in their behavior, such as sniffing glue or injuring themselves in a drunk-driving accident, their disability is a heavy enough burden without the added imposition of being ousted from society.

Most of us who read books like this one believe we are firmly entrenched members of the Us group, or even of the elite Revered. Consider, for example, a young man who believes he is invulnerable in his youth and health, immune to ever being cast into Group 3. He has passed all the tests, has no impairments of vision, hearing, ambulation or cognition. He is self-assured that he has the "right" skin color, the "right" sexual orientation and the "right" religious affiliation.

But that could change. He could have a stroke that renders him paralyzed and inarticulate. He would then go, literally in a heartbeat, from his current status to that of being "disabled." Would he no longer be deserving of the same dignity, respect and courtesy to which he had become accustomed?

Perhaps the tragedy of being cast to the Outside comes home to us with greatest clarity when we think about the devalued group that many of us–regardless of our current competence, wealth or influence–may have the opportunity to join. It is the group we call "the elderly." We have special agencies for "them," hold social issues forums about "their" needs and commit "them" to places that may have all the characteristics of an institution.

If you think the philosophy of Universal Enhancement, of inclusion for all people, is something that has no application to your life, think again. We could all be Them one day, cast aside from the mainstream of community life. How they are treated, related to and supported is important to each of us.

TOOLBOX
Using Universal Language

It matters how we say it, so practice making these substitutions.

PREVIOUS LANGUAGE	PREFERRED LANGUAGE
Mentally retarded person	Person with intellectual disabilities
High-functioning	Smart, competent
Noncompliant	Doesn't like to do what is asked
Loading the van	Helping people board
Passing meds	Assisting people to take their medication
Wheelchair-bound	Uses a wheelchair
Admitted	Moved in
Discharged	Moved out
The disabled	People with disabilities
Feeding	Assisting people to eat
Work the floor	Engage with people
Normal	Typical
Non-am	Unable to walk
Tube feeder	Receives nourishment by tube
Low functioning	Dependent, requires extensive support

Avoid words like "unfortunate," "afflicted" and "victim." People can have disabilities without being victimized by them.

It Matters How We Say It

It matters how we say it because what we say influences and communicates how we think. And if we think that people who are different from Us belong in a separate group from "the rest of us," they will. Their separation further isolates them, keeps them from knowing us and us from knowing them, reinforces our stereotypes and prejudices, and erects a wall of fear and mistrust. Our opportunities to develop the relationships that compel us to treat Them with respect and dignity will be diminished. If we cast people aside, we will never be able to work actively to remove the barriers that constantly stymie their attempts at being with the rest of us. We will maintain the role of Gatekeeper, keeping ourselves In and "the others" Out.

If the gates remain closed and the barriers remain in place, They will never learn how to live with Us, either. People who have failed some element of the contrived tests of life will learn only from each other if forced to live and interact with "their own kind." They will simply learn to perpetuate the behaviors that resulted in their failing the test in the first place. They will learn only to rock and make strange noises and ignore the other people in the park.

It does matter how we say it, for how we say it reflects how we see it. And how we see it–our expectation–determines how we will act. If we can see and speak a vision of inclusion for all people, we will be well on the way to being a force for Universal Enhancement.

2

Two Visits and Some Observations

You can see it from a long way off. The tall, brick chimney rises above the horizon. It is a marker, a beacon. As you get closer, you see the water tower with the words "State School and Hospital" inscribed boldly and proudly. It is obviously not a prison since it has no bars, guard towers or razor wire. In fact, the long winding drive leading visitors to the main building (where the flagpoles are) looks like the welcoming approach to a country estate of some wealthy railroad baron from the early 1900s. The grounds are artfully landscaped and neatly maintained. You have difficulty finding a place to park in the large lots, which remind you of your last trip to a shopping mall. You park near the building called "Creekside," and are greeted by your guide for the day.

On entering the first residential building, you realize immediately that this complex of structures is not a country estate. All your senses suddenly stand at alert in response to the barrage of strange incoming messages. The first thing you notice–it cannot be avoided–is the smell. It is a strange amalgam of body secretions and the chemicals used by staff to clean and cover the stench.

Then the noise strikes you. As your guide escorts you through the halls, you notice that she must raise her voice to be heard above the echoes that reverberate from a maze of hard surfaces–plaster, cement block, terrazzo, Plexiglass and fiberglass. It is a reverberant racket, a din of indistinguishable sounds. The guide does not seem to notice either the smell or the noise. People who work here become habituated to this deafening environment. When they return home, their families sometimes ask, "Why are you shouting?"

Your guide takes you down long hallways, past doors with names or instructions on them–Pharmacy, Training Lab, Day Activity Room, Staff Only, and WARNING: Automatic Doors.

What is going on here? You see people sitting in wheelchairs in the hallways, parked seemingly at random. Other people sit on well-worn, yellow fiberglass benches, rocking back and forth. Others are lying on the hard, cold terrazzo floor studying the flickering movements of

their own hands against the glare of overhead fluorescent lights. Some, who are only partially clothed, seem to take no notice of their nakedness. Others wear clothes that look like they have been constructed from the lines of some archetypal clothing pattern, the assorted shirts and pants distinguishable only by their variety of pastel colors and the "cottage" names written boldly on the backs with laundry markers.

Now you see someone wearing a name tag and a uniform smock "towing" an elderly, disheveled-looking man through this maze of clutter as if he were so much freight. They are going someplace, but neither of them seems happy about it. Their faces show no emotion at all. You pass a row of toilets, lined up like porcelain teeth with no dividers between them, no toilet paper, no seats, some flushed and some not. You are glad no one is using them as you pass. It would have been embarrassing.

On your way from one building to another, you notice the stark contrast again–the charming, bucolic exterior and the prison-like interior. The hills beyond the fence are a distant place, reachable only through "elopement" or a "home visit." You are glad your home is down the highway, back in what you are starting to view as "the real world."

The staff people in the next building are bustling back and forth, carrying piles of linen, trays of food and stacks of papers. Everybody seems to be doing something, but it is difficult to determine the purpose of all the activity, because life here is so different from the life you know back home in your town. The ordinary touchstones, social units, positive rituals and natural rhythms of life that you take for granted are missing. You cannot get any sense of reliable patterns or meaningful standards in this place.

The homey, daily events–sharing the evening meal, lowering the volume on the TV set to answer the telephone, or waiting until your teenage daughter gets out of the bathroom–are missing. The usual preferred activities–hobbies and interests that would reveal the individuality of the people who live here–have been replaced with schedules. They tell a tale, not of unique human beings, but of the regularized rhythms of a mass of people forced to live together with no sense of affinity or belonging.

Even the relationships seem hierarchical rather than reciprocal. It is clear who makes the decisions here–the people who carry the keys and wear the name badges. They manage, supervise and direct. They have access to all the rooms, the equipment and the outside world.

You also notice that everybody seems to be waiting for something. They are waiting for someone to signal that it is lunchtime by unlocking the day room door. They are waiting for someone to get the matches, a signal that it is time to go out and have a cigarette. They

Facilities are meant to be flushed, not lived in.

are waiting for the nurse to call their names for "med pass." Some may just be waiting for the end of the day to come, so they can go back to bed. What a life!

You are in an institution, for sure.

Workers in the Vineyard

I sincerely hope my intent in painting such an unflattering picture of this place is not misunderstood. I am not in any way criticizing the people who are working here. I have worked here, and I know by heart the good, honest, caring people who struggle in this place for some dignity for themselves and those they care for. They go home to their families smelling of this place, the din still reverberating in their heads. They do the best they can. They love the people they serve here. They cry when someone dies and take joy in small successes. They are the workers in this bizarre vineyard, reaping what harvest they can.

The people who work in this place, like those who live here, are also *institutionalized*. They have to leave a little part of themselves at the door when they come to work, and unfortunately, it is often the part that is most human.

Another Visit

The place I have just described is a collage of the large, state-operated facilities that dot the land all across this country. But let us visit another home for Outsiders, one that does not look anything like the isolated campus with the chimney and the water tower.

This new place is a neat brick home on a quiet residential street in a small town, maybe your town. You can tell it is different from your house because it has a large paved area around back where a van with a wheelchair lift is parked. But, the house is the same size as the other houses on the block, and has a neatly landscaped yard with a patio and barbecue grill out back.

When you ring the front doorbell, a pleasant-looking lady answers and welcomes you. Inside, the place is neat and clean, kept that way by the nice lady and her coworkers, who are proud of their "group home." They introduce you to the "residents," sitting around on the comfortable furniture. Some sit facing the TV set located in a wood-grained media center in the little living room.

A young man is rocking back and forth, making a repetitive moaning sound. A woman wearing some kind of football helmet approaches, wraps her arms around you and says, "How old are you? Are you married?"

Group Home

Oxymoron – Families and individuals live in homes, not groups.

Your hostess directs the woman to "leave the nice man alone." She steers you to the bedrooms. There are three on either side of a hallway, located at one end of the house. This one has Eric's name on the door and his Special Olympics ribbon tucked into a corner of the framed picture of red-coated men hunting with hounds. A caring staff person has neatly made the single bed. The room next door has the same color scheme, curtains and bedspread as Eric's, but it belongs to Julie. There are no pictures on the wall because "she tears them up." Your guide tells you the other rooms are "pretty much the same."

You drank too much coffee on your trip up here, so you ask the lady in charge to direct you to the bathroom. She points out the Staff Bathroom next to the coat closet in the hall and confides, "I don't think you'd want to use the other ones." The staff bathroom is as clean as the rest of the house, smelling heavily of disinfectant. You notice that, unlike the empty resident bathrooms, there is a stack of old magazines by the toilet and a roll of fresh toilet paper hanging nearby.

It is immediately obvious which persons are staff and which are residents. The staff are running the home, proud of it, welcoming to visitors and dressed to impress. The residents sit about doing little until

Support staff should be a quiet voice in the background

told by their "keepers" that it is time for some scheduled activity or program. The people living in this bungalow in a lovely neighborhood look remarkably like those you saw at the state hospital. But, this is not an institution; it is a group home. You even had trouble finding the place because no sign out front identified it as a "facility."

It's What's Inside That Counts.

··

These are merely a facade.

Mobile home in a park	High rise in the city
Farm in a rural area	A-frame in the woods
Ranch house in the suburbs	Cabin in the mountains
Brownstone in the inner city	Cottage on the lake

We all want to live in the same place: a place where we are treated with DIGNITY and RESPECT.

Signs are one of the differentiating factors we use to separate institutions from private residences. Institutions have names like "Autumn Acres Rest Home," "Senior Citizens Apartments" or "Social Services Halfway House." Your own home may have a sign on it, but it probably says something like "The Flannerys." Your sign proclaims to all that it is your home, the place where you live. Any other kind of sign says it is an institution, a place where people work. This place, this home, must be okay, because there is no sign. But, remember who answered the door.

The fact that a staff person greeted you when you rang the doorbell gives you some indication of whose home this really is. You realize that throughout the tour, you got no real sense of who the residents are. You, on the other hand, present yourself through your home. How you live in your home, how you decorate it and the types of objects you choose and keep around yourself all proclaim who you are. What your home tells me about you affects the way I relate to you.

> **MAXIM:** *"Group home" is an oxymoron.*

The things you have seen in the group home tell you that the people who live there are not important or individuals; they are really just assignments, "work units" like the sweatshirts one staff person used to sew for a living at a factory. This lack of individuality–the absence of the clues that tell you the people who live here have a life–may make you wonder whether the term "group home" is not an oxymoron. Home is not a place for groups; it is a place for family, a place for individuals.

Not a Place

We need to be careful that we are not fooled by the outward appearance of a place. The absence of the physical characteristics we expect in an "institution" can beguile us into thinking we have left that awful place behind. But such enchantment is insidious. It lulls us into a smug sense of "progress," so we do not see that some very significant aspects of life are the same in this group home as they were in the state-operated facility.

We need to observe vigilantly what is actually happening. We must attend more to the characteristics of life and interaction than to the architecture of the buildings, and recognize that "an institution is not a place; it is a state of mind."

> **MAXIM:** *An institution is not a place; it is a state of mind.* ™

It does not matter that a residence is right in town, sided in vinyl, and filled with people who have been "deinstitutionalized." What matters is the mindset of the people inside–those who see themselves as "staff" (that is, people paid to be there), and those who are considered "consumers" or "clients" (that is, guests of a sort, who are there to be *taken care of* or *serviced*).

"Nosocomial" Behavior

An amazing thing about the institutional mindset is that it stifles ambition. People who live in environments where they have no need to initiate meaningful activity because staff do it for them do not try to meet their own everyday needs. They do not take responsibility for their lives.

The recipients of constant staff "care" soon learn not to care for themselves in another way. They do not appreciate themselves, or see themselves as valuable and valued people. And when this happens, it is only natural that they no longer appreciate or value anyone else, either.

People who live amid shifts and chores, surveys and "care for" learn to fit right in. They become dependent, which is to say "lazy;" or they might even become aggressive or rebellious, in other words "noncompliant." People who are cared for regularly can easily fall into a state of "learned helplessness," sitting back and waiting for someone to do something to, or for, them.

Do you think those behaviors are a symptom of their condition? Were the people you saw in the State School and Hospital who sat, rocked and made weird noises doing so because they have intellectual disabilities? Well, think again. Look at the people who live in the institutions we call "nursing homes," "convalescent centers," "sanatoriums" or "psychiatric hospitals." They are also pacing, wringing their hands and vocalizing meaninglessly. People who live in institutional settings–environments where life is purposeless and meaningless–all respond to those characteristics similarly, with purposeless, meaningless behavior.

Isn't that amazing? Maybe there is some kind of common gene or enzyme deficiency in people over the age of eighty, people with schizophrenia, and people with an IQ below seventy. Or, (and this is a very important "or") the places where these people live cause bizarre and alienating behaviors. We call it "nosocomial" behavior.

The term comes from the Greek *nosos* (disease) and *komein* (to care for). A nosocomial disease is caused by being cared for; that is, it is contracted in the hospital. Likewise, nosocomial behavior is caused by the nature and quality of treatment a person receives. The behavior is a person's response to the service system, established by the paid staff, the Gatekeepers, the people from Group 2. And therein lies a tale, a tale to be told in the rest of this book.

Characteristics of the Institutional State of Mind

Let us examine some of the characteristics that make up the institutional state of mind. We do so because we need to learn to recognize and sensitize ourselves to the indicators and implications of the almost-hidden attributes of institutional settings. Unless we know the institutional characteristics so well that they leap into our awareness, they will slip into our lives unnoticed and sabotage our best efforts at reform.

This process is similar to one an experienced outdoorsman would use when explaining to a novice how to find wild mushrooms in the woods. The outdoorsman would encourage the novice by saying, "Put on your mushroom eyes. Once you know the characteristics of the mushrooms–their size, shape and color–your eyes will take over. When you're wearing your mushroom eyes, you will see mushrooms everywhere."

The person who was inexperienced in the ways of the woods stood looking around, unable to see even a single mushroom on the leaf-littered floor of the woods. After a while, though, as the novice drew the images of mushrooms into his mind and relaxed into the process, mushrooms seemed to sprout under every tree. Drifts and caches of mushrooms of several varieties appeared before this new wearer of "mushroom eyes." And a wonderful mushroom lunch was had by all.

When I visit a place while wearing my "institutional characteristics eyes," troubling scenes seem to abound. Interactions that pass unnoticed by the staff–that seem to them just part of the everyday routine–jump into my awareness as powerful indicators of relationships that need attention. Items that are not age appropriate stand out like an upside-down owl in a "What's wrong with this picture?" puzzle. The use of a term like "low functioning" grates on the ear like the vilest curse word.

Though a well-developed set of "institutional characteristics eyes and ears" might bring you the reputation of being a picky troublemaker, you must be willing to develop and apply them. This process is called *advocacy*. Only if you are willing to raise your standard to the level of asking, "Is this the kind of place where I would like to live?" will you begin to see the hazards, deficiencies and indecencies in an institutional environment.

When you ask, "Is this the kind of *place* where I'd like to live?" you should consider not only the new, well-equipped kitchen, the nice furniture and the big TV with a built-in DVD player. Those things make the place very desirable, but what about the *state of mind* that permeates it? Would you be willing to sacrifice your privacy, autonomy and adult freedoms for the sake of a new microwave oven? Hardly.

MAXIM: *Our Standard: Is this the kind of place where I would want to live?*

I am embarrassed to admit that I used to think of the question in terms of, "Is this the kind of place where I would like to live... if I had an intellectual disability?" But, that is like asking whether this is the kind of place I would like to live if I were Puerto Rican, blonde or Jewish.

We must strongly challenge the notion that there can be different life standards for different "classes" of human beings.

> **Characteristics of the Total Institution**
>
> 1. Remote from the mainstream of society
> 2. Lack of privacy
> 3. Lack of individualization
> 4. Restriction on freedom of movement
> 5. Disabilities viewed in a medical context
> 6. Environment denies dignity of opportunity/risk
> 7. The least restrictive alternative is determined by the person with the most impairment
> 8. Individuals seen in childlike imagery
> 9. Choice and decision-making are restricted
> 10. Large group functions

TALE
Watch Out for 'De'

Sometimes you can enter a place where Outsiders reside, or a special place that serves their needs like sheltered workshops. I've been there many times.

And, I can often sense an alien presence there, an evil, sinister force. On the rare occasion when I have glimpsed this evil being, he has appeared as a tiny person, dressed in a black cloak and hat, his threatening eyes almost hidden. His name is "De."

Though it is hard to catch a glimpse of this menacing being, sometimes you can smell him. De smells like stale urine and cheap disinfectant.

Though he has no voice of his own, De can be heard in talk that is directed to Outsiders. You can hear him in the parental tone of voice the staff uses: "Put that down!" "Where are you going?" "Leave that alone!" "Come here!" And, De can be heard in the childlike tone of voice the staff uses: "Does Sammy want to peel apples with us? C'mon. Do it for Miss Katie?"

There are many ways you can sense De, but he is usually hidden. He hides under beds, in closets or cupboards, or under the furthest rear seat of the fifteen-passenger van.

De's presence is frequently subtle. He usually appears by attaching himself to the beginning of many words; and once he does that, he won't let go.

When he attaches himself to the word "value," it becomes "Devalue." When he connects with the word "meaning," it is transformed suddenly into "Demeaning." If he catches hold of "grade," "Degrade" makes an appearance. Even "humanize" becomes "Dehumanize," when De takes over.

Watch out for De, people. He's in your home, on your block and in your workplace. He's ready to grab your words, twist your values and ruin the lives of all he touches.

Only by focusing on the problems inherent in the institutional mindset can we begin to see the solutions, the tools we can use to make amends for the ways De has taken people's lives away from them, all in the name of "care." All the conditions that are institutional only occur because of the ways that people treat other people. De is found in our behavior.

Ten Characteristics to Be on Alert For

Institutional characteristics are infinite in number and various in appearance and impact. New characteristics take shape and evolve, as paradigms of treatment, support and service shift. What follows is an exploration of ten representative characteristics shared by institutional settings, whether they are group homes, nursing homes, orphanages, tuberculosis sanatoriums or prisons.

I would like to challenge you, as you read about these characteristics, to use them as benchmarks for your place of employment or the nursing home where your aunt lives or the "model" treatment center on the other side of town. When you use the new eyes developed through an awareness of the elements on this list, you will be amazed at the unsuspected locales where institutional characteristics lurk.

Remote from the Mainstream

By "remote" I am not merely referring to geographic distance, though their physically remote location is one of the more obvious characteristics of the large, government-operated, residential facilities we think of as "institutions." Indeed, the water tower and smokestack that greeted us during our initial visit suggested that many of these places were not

even provided with city utilities because of their distance from town. They generated their own power and supplied their own water. It is as though the umbilical cord that attached them to the ongoing life energy of the rest of the community had been severed.

The institution is designed to be self-contained and self-sufficient, so that no one from the community at large, except the people who work there, must ever visit or interact with the people who live there.

Lack of Privacy

Do not give people privacy... teach them to take it.

- ✓ Verbally prompt.
- ✓ Physically cue.
- ✓ Physically prompt.
- ✓ Provide graduated guidance.

None of the familiar and important community figures is ever present. All of the usual people are absent–the mail carrier, meter reader, garbage collector, Girl Scout selling cookies, newspaper delivery person, Lion's Club volunteer selling brooms, and Halloween trick-or-treater. The institution is a world unto itself, isolated and segregated.

But, a residence can be remote from the community mainstream even if it is located on a shady lot in the middle of our town. If the Welcome Wagon did not stop by to bring potholders, calendars and tire service coupons to the new people when they moved in, the place begins to take on the institutional shroud of remoteness.

If the new residents of the neighborhood did not go down to the post office to let the mail carrier know where they should get their mail, they probably will never receive any of the intriguing catalogs addressed to "John Jones or Current Resident." Nor will they get any "Welcome to the Neighborhood" solicitations from the local dentist or chiropractor.

If staff go to the grocery store while the residents of the home are at a work training program, the grocery store clerks will never know that Edward needs help with a grocery cart but likes to weigh the bananas. If it is easier to have Susie's sister come to the home to cut Eddie's hair (because the last time he visited the barber shop, he yelled, cried and tried to bite the barber), a little piece of remoteness develops.

If medications are delivered in locked fishing tackle boxes by uniformed express drivers, none of the home's residents will be seen hanging around at the condom display rack while they wait for the pharmacist to fill their prescription.

If eight-inch letters proclaim the agency name on the side of the van, the people who live in that house and ride in the vehicle parked in that driveway will be seen as separate, as They. If these and other distancing factors are present, the neighbors will see the new people on the block as part of an organization that is from the Outside. They will not make the effort needed to break through the barriers and establish relationships. It happens by degrees, subtly. Soon, that new house in town may as well sprout a smokestack and a water tower. It has become as remote as an institution.

Lack of Privacy

The institutional setting tends to structure most of life's activities to occur in groups, masses of people all doing the same thing at the same time. When groups of people live together, it is very difficult to protect and support personal privacy. Only through extended, asserted efforts is there anything like private space or time. People residing in

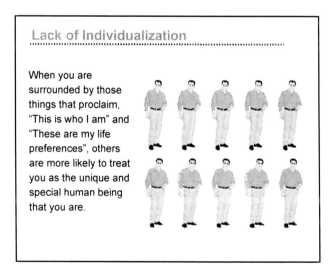

Lack of Individualization

When you are surrounded by those things that proclaim, "This is who I am" and "These are my life preferences", others are more likely to treat you as the unique and special human being that you are.

> **Individualization: Speaking Out**
>
> Decreased competence and capability increase the importance of individualization in one's life.
> - When a person is challenged in advocating for his/her interests, preferences and relationships, his/her belongings and artifacts serve as his/her voice.
> - Having "things" of value in one's life proclaims, I have a valued life and I am valued!"
>
>

institutional settings carry out most activities in the presence of others, and often either learn not to care about privacy issues or discover how to shut others out mentally. That is, they pretend to occupy a private world of their own making.

When all the basic functions of life, such as eating, sleeping, smoking, bathing and going to the toilet, occur as group activities, privacy may be easily lost in the shuffle. Privacy loses both relevance and importance in such a setting. A person who is accustomed to using the toilet with six other people, in bathrooms with no dividing partitions, curtains or doors between them, never develops a sense of privacy. As a result, she will certainly have no qualms about pulling down her pants in a parking lot and urinating in public. She has become habituated to doing so.

A person who eats regularly at a table set for twelve will have difficulty showing respect for the privacy of diners seated nearby in a restaurant. A person who has staff entering his bedroom without knocking, whose activities are checked at all hours, who showers with the assistance of strangers, and who has no safe place to be alone can hardly be expected to close doors behind himself or respect the closed doors–the privacy–of others.

The concept of privacy and the skills needed to achieve it are learned. We were not born with them. A person who has lived long years in an institutional setting is not likely to have learned much about privacy. That is why, in training sessions we conduct with staff, we say, "Don't give people privacy." We insist the trainees write it down as if it were a rule, a company policy. We ask them how it feels to be asked not to give people privacy. Then, we complete the statement with: "Teach them to take it."

So how do we teach people to take their privacy? Suppose, for example, a staff person, or even a caring friend or relative, accompanies someone to the bathroom because that person needs assistance and support. Then, in an attempt to demonstrate that he or she is "caring for" the person who needs to use the bathroom, the assisting person closes the bathroom door behind them. Our response to the support person is likely to be, "I'm glad you know how to close the bathroom door." But, instead of taking care of a person's privacy needs for him, the significant others in that person's life ought to approach going to the bathroom as a "teachable moment." The helper should recognize the opportunity to use cues, prompts and reinforcement to help the person learn how and when privacy is important.

Giving people privacy is a denial of rights, for it does not allow them the opportunity and dignity of learning how to create privacy for themselves.

Teaching a person to take advantage of his right to privacy involves employing a hierarchy of prompts that ranges from the least to the most intrusive. The relative, friend or direct support professional helping someone go to the bathroom might respond as follows:

1. Verbal prompt: "Bob, did you forget something?"

2. Verbal prompt with a physical cue: (Helper points to the door.) "Bob, did you forget something?"

3. Physical prompt: "Bob, did you forget something?" (Helper points to the door and touches Bob's arm.)

4. Physical prompt with hand-over-hand assistance: "Bob, can I help you close the bathroom door?" (Don't ask him to close the door because this encourages learned helplessness. Avoid taking over the function of the person's frontal lobe.)

MAXIM: *Don't give people privacy; teach them to take it.*

The reason privacy is so important is that it is a manifestation of courtesy. We do not interrupt "regular" people, listen in on their conversations or look into their windows. Thus, people who have never had this right respected nor learned to respect it with others will almost certainly be seen as Outsiders. Respecting the privacy of another is one of the hallmarks that someone is one of Us.

Lack of Individualization

People who live in an institution tend to do most things together and in the same manner. They arise from sleep at the same time. They wear similar clothing, carry the same lunch pails (with their name and "unit" emblazoned on the outside), and eat the same food at the same table. They take "smoke breaks" in groups, line up to go to the bathroom and do everything according to a schedule (haircut time, bath time, exercise time, chore time, learning time and work time).

This routinization, this lack of individuality, sounds like a description of prison or the army. That is because the army and prison are both institutions. So are prep school and medical school. Institutions, by their very nature, limit individualization in order to facilitate attainment of the institution's purpose or mission. The army (or any other branch of the military) must preserve "good order and discipline." It has "units" that are supposed to act as just that—one thing, one element that will take its place in the general plan. There is little room for individual difference in such a common purpose.

A prison limits individualization as punishment (no one likes it), and to protect the safety of the inmates and guards. Schools limit individualization for the "higher purpose" of assuring that everyone in the class learns the things they are going to need to know in order to graduate. In these instances, conformity is consciously applied as a means to achieving the institutional mission, and people volunteer to be subjected to it. Institutions for Outsiders have no such agreed-upon goal, and the inmates are seldom volunteers.

A basic tenet of our culture is that individuality should be respected. Most of Us are never required to earn the right to be treated as individuals, as the unique and special persons we are. So, why is a person who is perceived as deviating in a negative way from normative expectations required to sacrifice his or her individuality to the institution?

One reason for this mandated sacrifice is that a person's individuality may be seen as troublesome or even dangerous. The desire to pour milk on your chocolate cake and stir it up, walk around barefoot, or to stay up late at night and sleep in the morning are seen as challenges to the system.

Institutions for people with disabilities feel a need to maintain an order and discipline–similar to that imposed by military groups–as a way of "managing" people. Small numbers of staff can herd a large group of residents from one place to another at appointed times. But, any person's request to do something different from the group activity, or at a different time, would most likely be denied because "there are not enough staff."

This lack of opportunity to act on one's preference to either join in or skip whatever is planned for the group occurs as a result of limited resources, not as a means of realizing some wider, organizational objective. This scenario is not rare; too often, a person with intellectual disabilities spends much of his or her time waiting to participate in the staff's routines rather than being provided the opportunity to establish and develop a routine and schedule of his or her choosing.

Worst of all, individualization is restricted or absent because Outsiders are often not seen as individuals; they are stereotyped. How often have we heard, "This building is for the non-ams," or "The next group in here are the higher functioning." We are meeting not with individuals, but groups and classifications, diagnoses and stereotypes. Grouping allows us to focus on the perceived similarities among the people being grouped, rather than seeing either their commonalities with us or the uniqueness that makes them who they are.

As soon as we allow ourselves to see someone as part of They, as in "They like to go bowling" or "They defecate in the pool," there is little chance for a member of the group to be treated as an individual. Prejudicial grouping creates a self-fulfilling prophecy. People who are not appreciated and supported as unique individuals will conform more and more to the group expectations. They lose those characteristics that make them unique individuals, and end up looking more and more like the undifferentiated multitude they were predicted to be. Individuality is one of the things that make life worth living. Being treated as an individual and treating others as individuals enhances the quality of our lives.

The fabric of individuality is woven from a host of wonderful things that express a person's interests, hobbies, color preferences, significant others or spiritual preference, and so on. A mezuzah on the front door, a cluster of framed photos on the mantle, a much-played CD collection, a family tree, a frayed teddy bear–these are the kinds of objects that announce the presence of a unique and valuable person.

TALE
My Butterfly

We were out walking with a young man who uses a wheelchair for mobility, needs assistance and support with most of his daily tasks, and speaks not a word. As we proceeded down the sidewalk, a monarch butterfly flitted across our course.

We stopped, and I watched the young man attempt to follow the butterfly's erratic flight with his eyes. He grinned and made a sound of gladness.

When we returned to his home, I assisted him in cutting out the form of a butterfly from a piece of shirt cardboard. We then propped it up on the shelf in his bedroom.

Now, whenever I come to visit, he lets me know by a gesture of his head that he would like me to come to his room. When we get there, he directs his eyes toward the butterfly cutout, grins and makes a sound of gladness at our special shared event–his butterfly.

When people are surrounded by those things that proclaim their interests, it is more likely that others will treat them as the individual human beings they are. Singular attributes proclaim the presence of an individual person. And if we do not see the person, the opportunity to have a relationship with him or her is significantly diminished. We do not have relationships with groups or characteristics; we have relationships with individual people, people with whom we can share ourselves.

MAXIM: *The more people are surrounded by the things that proclaim who they are and what they are about, the more likely others will treat them as the unique and special human beings they are.*

When institutional pressures replace these expressions of individuality with environments that manifest a bleak and empty sameness, there is no way for us to see who is living there. And where we see no individuals, we see no life.

TALE
The Marathon Man
by Bob Williams

Johnny ran
that was his problem
he was what the staff called a runner
logical since he ran whenever he could

one minute they thought they had him
three ways to Sunday
tied to the bedpost
with someone else's soiled sheets
then they'd no sooner turn around
and he'd be up to his harry houdini
routine all over again

even the aides admitted he was pretty
smart for being a retard
all the rest of them would sit and rock

but not Johnny
he'd jump up
dart this way and that

then next thing you know
he'd find an open door
or leap through a window
and he'd be clocking the mile
on the institution's main drag
at three-point-ninety-two
like the long distance runner
he longed to be

they tried vinegar spray
four-point restraints
even leaden shoes

nothing slowed his free stride
until they placed electrodes on his hide
and shocked him
shocked him silly

now he's on the back ward
rocking to and fro
to and fro
to and fro

Restriction on Freedom of Movement

Among the paradigmatic symbols of the institution is the door key, an institutional icon as noteworthy as the smokestack and the water tower. Those in charge have the keys and therefore control.

Institutional authority figures often carry their keys prominently on a large ring attached by a short piece of chain to their belt loops. Even the sound of this wad of keys denotes authority and access. In today's downsized institutions, keys tend more often to be "master keys," worn stylishly on a brightly colored loop of something that looks like telephone cord. But the intent and impact is the same. Those who have keys–literal Gatekeepers–have the freedom to move about the place; those without must content themselves with the allowed areas, permissible times and acceptable activities. Those who have no keys must request access from those who do.

Restriction of freedom of movement has given rise to the common use of the term "AWOL" (absent without official leave) in many institutional settings. AWOL is a military term, originating from the legitimate military concern that everyone be present in order to carry out the organization's mission. Civilians do not go AWOL. Unfortunately, the currently popular institutional euphemism "to elope" is no better. Most people think of elopement as what young people do when they run off to get married without their parents' permission. That is one definition of the word. The other definition is "to run away, to escape." Institutions write policies for dealing with someone who elopes, an "escapee." This institutional policy that forbids residents to leave is one that should cause discomfort in those of us who cherish our own freedom.

The concept of needing permission in order to be absent leads to a whole range of restrictions that are simply taken for granted by those who accept, without questioning, the standards of the institution. Staff see themselves as justified in telling people where they can go, when they can go and how long they can stay. This even includes establishing bedtimes and telling residents how long they have to stay in bed.

Restriction of freedom of movement is also expressed in the directive tone of some institutional staff: "Put that down," "Come here" and "Leave that alone." This type of command–what we call "barking"–is designed to manage and control. It emanates from staff who see themselves as occupying the Us circle and see the people they serve as belonging with the Outsiders.

When we see persons we are employed to support as individuals with lives and not merely as patients, clients, consumers who need treatment, or children who need protection, we see restrictions on freedom as serious human rights issues. Once we have this awareness, we will realize that any place with internally key-locked doors is a prison, unless you are one of the privileged persons who carry a key. We will see that our denying someone the right to come and go as they choose puts us in the role of oppressor and the restricted one in the role of oppressed.

Why should some individuals—because of personal attributes and qualities that are beyond their power to change—lose their right to gather with those people they like, move about from place to place, stay home from work today, or get up at 2:00 a.m. to watch television because they cannot sleep?

TALE
So, What's the Problem?

I got a call from a home manager one day saying he had "a problem." It seems a woman who lived in the home where he worked kept getting up at 1:30 in the morning.

"How often does she do this?" I asked.

"Three or four nights a week," he answered.

"What does she do when she gets up?"

"She goes into the kitchen," he replied.

"What does she do in the kitchen?"

"She makes a cup of hot chocolate."

"What does she do with it?"

"She takes it into the living room."

"What does she do there?"

"She turns on the television."

"Does she turn it on loud enough to bother other people in the house?"

"No."

"How long does she stay up?"

"Sometimes as long as an hour or two."

"Then what does she do?"

"She goes back to bed."

"How old is she?"

"Thirty-five."

"So what's the problem?"

Of course, we give lip service to the principle of freedom. We have "civil rights reviews," "due process" and "human rights committees." But, these functions are usually part of the system–they are mandated by regulation. The people designated to be rights watchdogs may still have bought into the notion that Outsiders are different enough from other people that they can therefore be seen as having a different set of rights.

They may find acceptable ways to justify prohibiting "residents" from entering "the staff office." Or, they may approve policies that require us to bring back a person who "eloped"–that is, who went over the fence to see the wildflowers or pet the neighbor's horse, even though the person was in no immediate danger.

No one should have "different" rights simply by dint of manifesting a condition that has marked him or her as an Outsider.

Of course, having rights is not the same as having unlimited options, sometimes expressed as "doing whatever I want." Though we all have rights, our options are always bounded by a consideration of other people's rights. Some people's rights (as well as their options) are abridged *as a result of their actions and choices.* Convicted felons, for example, may lose the right to own firearms or vote in elections. The key word here is "convicted." Our constitutional principles

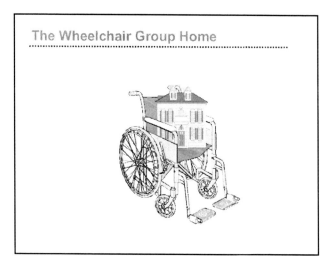

The Wheelchair Group Home

require that no citizen's rights can be limited "without due process of law." Someone who loses rights because of having been convicted of a crime has had this due process assured by the courts.

This constitutional protection applies even to people labeled as Outsiders. But many Outsiders lose their rights through the process of diagnosis or the court of public opinion. They have never been tried or convicted. They have only been sentenced.

We should evaluate restrictions on freedom of movement in the same way we evaluate our speech in Universal Language. That is, we should ask ourselves whether this is an activity people in Group 2 –Us–would be allowed to do. Or, is being AWOL a "status offense"? That is, if a person were not a resident of the institution (diminished status), would she be "allowed" to go to a particular area? Are staff allowed to go there?

We are often met with a look of confused shock when we ask a group of staff trainees (people new to the business of offering supports and services) whether a person with a significant intellectual disability who lives in a group home, has no intelligible speech, and needs help with his "toileting hygiene" has the right to go down to the corner bar and watch the St. Patrick's Day parade on TV with his buddies. They have never thought of "letting" someone like that do such a thing.

Clearly, they are trapped in the old paradigm, believing their job is to control and protect. They think people with disabilities are "not ready" for real life situations that commonly bring us pleasure and participation. They cannot yet see how their own lives would be enhanced if they could be supports instead of guards.

Disabilities as Medical Issues

In many institutional settings serving people with intellectual disabilities, the people in charge have credentials in health care fields. They are MDs, RNs, OTs, PTs and LPNs. Even the "direct care" staff often have medically-oriented titles. They are called "health care technicians," "nurse's aides" or "psychiatric assistants." A person living in an institution that is structured this way is usually called "patient."

Information about their condition and progress is maintained in "charts." They are "admitted," "discharged" and "staffed." "Doctor's orders" are just that, orders from on high, meant to be carried out by obedient subordinates. As was stated in Chapter 2, intellectual disability is not a disease. People with intellectual disabilities are not afflicted with a sickness or an illness.

Of course, some intellectual disabilities are caused by medical conditions such as Phenylketonuria, Rh incompatibility or hydrocephalus, disorders for which early medical intervention may be crucial. Unfortunately, by the time these conditions have resulted in an intellectual disability and accompanying dysfunction, they seldom respond to additional medical treatment or interventions to reverse the neurological damage that was exacted.

A person with an intellectual disability may also have a medical condition, such as a seizure disorder, visual impairment, a cut knee or a stuffy nose. The person may need medical assistance with these medical problems, as do the rest of us. But, the person's intellectual disability does not require any medical treatment in itself.

When a person who has been cast Outside is diagnosed as also having conditions that require medical treatment, any such diagnosis is neither an invitation nor a sanction for a health care provider to control and manage the person's life. No action is required beyond the extent they might act on behalf of anyone who had that medical condition. To understand this better, think about what would happen if you were diagnosed as having severe hypertension and were forty pounds overweight. You would probably angrily reject the notion that this diagnosis gives your doctor the right to come into your home and throw away your salt and ice cream. You would be surprised if a nurse showed up at your door while you were enjoying your Sunday nap to take you on your required two-mile walk at a time she scheduled.

Seeing people with intellectual disabilities as sick has served to justify limiting their freedoms and making decisions for them. People are often "placed" in an institutional environment in order to receive "treatment." The tragedy is that, although the prescription is "admission for treatment," it too often becomes "admission as treatment." Once a person is admitted, he or she languishes in the sterile environment that was supposed to make him or her better.

Where medical personnel are in charge and the goal is treatment and "custodial care" (safekeeping), people are under the direction of the Medical/Custodial Model of services to people with disabilities. Pervasive and intrusive "care," which mandates the control of a person's entire life, is the hallmark of this model. It is based on the unequal doctor/patient relationship–a healer who has something to give and a patient who is deficient or lacking. It is a "do for" model, a model that nurtures learned helplessness. The person in the institution is deemed "in need of caretaking" as a result of his or her illness, and the "caretakers" are only too willing to fulfill that role.

The Medical/Custodial Model was the predominant standard of services for persons with developmental disabilities for decades. Many of the famous "innovators" in techniques for "treatment" of them were physicians. And, staff who served in chief supervisory roles were nurses. Those who worked with the patients were called "direct care" staff, because caring for people was their job assignment. Often, the training such staff received was modeled on the training of nursing home and hospital staff. The trainees learned to make beds, give enemas,

> **View I/DD in a Medical Context**
>
> An intellectual or developmental disability is not a disease. It is an adaptive disorder. A person with I/DD lacks the skills and abilities that we usually expect of a person at that age.
>
> *Yes, I think he has intellectual disability.*

measure blood pressure and document the patient's "condition" in "charts." Unfortunately, many aspects of this model of service delivery are far from extinct, for it still permeates many of today's practices.

The Medical/Custodial Model gave society at large the assurance that "the mentally deficient" were being humanely cared for while relieving communities of the responsibility of doing something with Them closer to their home. Placing people in institutions, where they could be adequately cared for, was justified as good for them and for the greater good of society. People with intellectual disabilities (or people with TB, leprosy, mental illness or AIDS) could be protected from the taunting and teasing or even out-and-out exploitation they would suffer if they were in their home communities.

But, locking people up–restricting and limiting their choices because they might be exploited–is like locking women up because they might be raped. It is much the same as putting an adolescent in a juvenile detention center because he ran away from an abusive home. It is what we did when we put Japanese-Americans in internment camps during World War II, in order to protect them from the rage of their prejudiced neighbors. Many of us participate in the decision to place elderly parents in "rest homes" because they might fall prey to con men or burglars in their own homes. But, protective incarceration punishes the victim rather than seeking to prevent the abuse.

The tragedy is that keeping a person away from the community—away from risk, relationships and opportunity—is like keeping the sick person in bed for an extended period. It is only in recent years that the practice of prescribing six to eight weeks of "bed rest" for recuperation from an illness has become known to contribute to, if not outright cause, a lot of the degenerative conditions for which it was once prescribed.

Likewise, the practice of restricting the opportunities of a person who has limited skills and abilities is exactly the opposite of what we should do to improve the quality of his or her life, and to ameliorate the severity of his or her limitations. A person who has an intellectual disability needs more opportunities, not fewer.

Environment Denies Dignity of Risk/Opportunity

When making decisions about how to design and structure support services, the following Trilogy of Service Principles is a helpful guide:
1. Protect from harm
2. Assure dignity and respect
3. Provide learning opportunities.

The principles are listed in priority order. In practice, however, we most often experience a conflict between the first and third. When such a conflict arises in an institution, priority is almost invariably given to protection from harm. This preference developed through a long history of negative consequences (investigations, punishment and public censure) when someone in an institutional environment "gets hurt."

The public outcry and personal consequences of apparent harm to a person receiving services outweigh a concern for the ongoing, pervasive harm that befalls any person who must live in institutional circumstances. Thus, those who work in institutional settings are really protecting themselves when they see their principal responsibility as protecting people from harm and minimizing risk. This pervasive (and invasive) concern with the possibility that "someone might get hurt" is an obvious artifact of the Medical/Custodial Model.

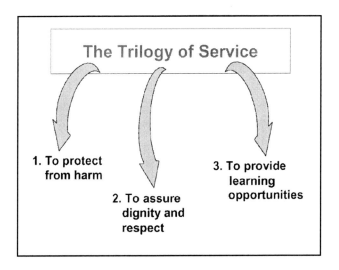

The old saying, attributed to Abraham Maslow, tells us that if the only tool you have is a hammer, you will see every problem as a nail. This is the concept of "functional fixedness." Likewise, if you staff a facility with a preponderance of doctors and nurses, there is a tendency to see most issues as medical. Doctors and nurses take an oath to "do no harm." If someone in an institution breaks his or her arm, there has been a failure of the system. An investigation will be initiated into the cause of the accident, and steps will be taken to see that it does not happen again.

Unfortunately, these steps might include removing the dangerous playground equipment; draining the swimming pool; replacing the stairs with ramps; requiring all persons with awkward gaits to wear protective equipment; assuring that no one is ever left unsupervised for even a few minutes; and on and on. After any sort of accidental injury, a sweeping effort often ensues, aimed at protecting from harm but resulting in the denial of many of life's precious opportunities.

If you did not grow up in an institution, your parents, though kind and loving people, probably decided to risk the possibility that you would break your neck and become permanently paralyzed. No? Did they let you crawl up a flight of steps? Did they let you swing on the swings? Did they allow you to ride a bicycle? Of course they did. Your parents balanced the risk that you might be injured with the necessity of providing you with opportunities to experience life and learn from those experiences. They knew you had to risk falling down if you were ever to walk.

In the interest of protection from harm, those who operate institutional settings often make decisions that remove opportunities. The use of spoons but no other utensils at mealtime removes the risk of people getting injured with forks and knives. But, it also removes the opportunity to learn how to cut a piece of chicken. Wearing clothes that have no pockets or buttons removes the risk of swallowing buttons or carrying contraband. But, such clothing also removes the opportunity to learn how to use pockets or button buttons. These are skills necessary for being able to dress in the kind of clothes that most people in our neighborhoods wear.

Residents of institutions do not operate stoves because they might get burned. They do not walk around town because they might get taunted by a cruel person passing by. The mandate to "care for" keeps people in bed, in helmets and indoors. The person who is kept entirely free from harm is not free to grow and learn; thus, he or she cannot learn many of the skills needed for having a life. As a result, the person remains dependent, infantile and ignorant. If they do happen to get near a stove, they are likely to burn themselves. If they cross the street, the blaring of horns pushes them back.

In short, if they have not been offered the same kind of limited, graduated risks our parents gave us as children, they will not win the dignity that we acquired by learning how to do new things. They will have been protected from becoming adult human beings and participating in "our" world.

We are not, of course, advocating foolish risk-taking. We need to understand the concept of "enlightened risk," the balancing of prudence with opportunity. We must ask ourselves the question, "Does the potential enhancement of this person's quality of life outweigh the possible risks we can foresee?" This should not be an unfamiliar consideration since the question is Universal. It is the same question we ask ourselves when assessing our own risky ventures. If the answer is that the potential enhancement does indeed outweigh the potential harm, we decide to go ahead. Such weighing is one of life's most difficult tasks.

Those of us who provide services or supports to another person often find ourselves in a position of making tricky judgments, sharing with that person the responsibility for an outcome. Our situation is

Learning Requires Risk

illustrated in the well-known figure of Lady Justice, standing blindfolded with her balance scale in hand. If we err on the side of safety, unwilling to permit enlightened risks, the person served misses important opportunities for some of life's most rewarding adventures. The scale is tipped too far to the side of "Responsibility." But, we soon come to understand that people who are denied the opportunity to experience risky life activities may actually be more at risk.

The person served ends up with few tools with which to protect himself or herself. The balance swings back toward the side of "Risk." If, however, we err too far on the side "Risk," serious injury or death may result and put an end to all opportunity. Lady Justice is blind; we cannot afford to be.

As we serve and support persons with intellectual disabilities, our need to constantly perform this delicate balancing act is one of our most difficult challenges. Particularly when we are offering supports to a person whose judgment is compromised by a disability, we will almost certainly err on the conservative side. If a person cannot fully understand the consequences of her actions, we are not likely to encourage the same kinds of risky ventures we might plan for ourselves. We take on a heavy load of responsibility when we make these decisions for others. But the load is spread considerably when it is shared with members of a team of people who approach the issue from various perspectives.

MAXIM: *Where there is no risk, there is no dignity.*

One of the riskiest ventures we all undertake in our lives is the development of relationships, especially intimate relationships. Friends sometimes betray us, and lovers may turn to someone new. We can be hurt in our hearts and souls. But, most of us decide that the great joy we get from sharing our lives with friends and loved ones is worth the risk that some of it might go sour.

Environment Denies Dignity of Opportunity- "Risk"

In environments where there is no risk, there is no dignity.

All learning requires risk.

Of course, some people, having been badly wounded in the relationship wars, withdraw from the field. They keep to themselves and decide not to risk their hearts again in such an uncertain venture. But even these battle-scarred veterans are deciding for themselves, based on information gained from risks already taken. When we take this option away from a person, thinking she might be hurt by love, we deny her an opportunity to experience one of life's greatest endeavors.

Where there is no risk, there is neither growth nor learning. Where there is no risk, there is no dignity. It is that simple. No one can learn new things, explore new territory, or develop new relationships without risk. The institution obliterates and prevents those opportunities by being overly concerned with its role as protector.

Least Restrictive Environment

This characteristic emerges primarily as a result of the staff's failure to discover innovative and creative solutions that provide protection from harm for the person who requires it, while offering opportunities to those who need them. It is much easier to restrict everyone than to develop ways to engineer an environment that is reasonably safe while still being rich in opportunities for engagement. Creeping restrictionism is an insidious process that turns institutional environments, wherever they may be found, into wastelands of locked cabinets, unbreakable furniture and plastic food trays.

No one ever plans a wasteland, of course; it just happens over time as a response to the impairments and challenges presented in each locale. The alternative is to find creative solutions to each difficult challenge. There can be no shortcuts, and no standardized solution that is imposed on all individuals.

In one institutional setting, for instance, we meet Clara who has outbursts during which she has sometimes thrown furniture. As a result, the furniture is now bolted to the floors and walls. A more creative alternative might be either lightweight, soft furniture or furniture that is too heavy to throw, though movable when necessary. In both cases, Clara should have the option of choosing the furniture. She is less likely to throw her own furniture.

Now consider George, who wandered off one night. It took six staff people an hour to find him, so now the doors are internally key locked. A more inventive solution would be to install a standard security system that sounds a warning when the door is opened. With this in place, George's support staff could engage him at the door and remind him that he forgot to let them know he wanted to go outside.

Sarah and B.J. "stole" unscheduled snacks from the refrigerator, so the refrigerator door was chained. But, this restriction proved to be a nuisance for everyone, so an imaginative support person helped them buy their own "snack boxes." They keep the boxes locked, thus practicing the shared value of "my belongings" and "your belongings".

One day, Bob was too cold so he turned the heat up. Now, the thermostat is behind a wire mesh covering. A creative alternative is to help Bob learn to read the thermometer and the thermostat. He could assume the role of heat monitor, keeping the temperature within an agreed-upon range.

While it is true that some restrictions must be made in the interest of safety and good order, too often they are made in the interest of administrative expediency. In response to the various challenging behaviors or impairing medical conditions experienced by each person receiving services, constraints are applied, which, taken together, can cause a multiplier effect. In a home shared by six people, for example, the sum of all limitations imposed by administrative response to each person's "inappropriate behavior" can be significant.

Imagine the effect where six *hundred* people live together. Any time groups of people live together under administrative regulations and restrictions, everyone's options are typically limited. Creative alternatives must be found so opportunities for learning and participation will not be denied.

Childlike Imagery

This is a perennial problem. Because people with disabling conditions are perceived as having the skills and abilities one usually associates with young children, they are, unfortunately, seen by many as "children in adult bodies." They are cooed over, petted, talked down to, and generally devalued and demeaned.

At one large, state-operated facility, the solemn brick building was divided into four living areas. The wards in these areas were called "Big Boys," "Little Boys," "Big Girls" and "Little Girls." There were very few children in those units. Indeed, some of the "little girls" were old enough to be mothers or grandmothers. They were put there, rather than on "Big Girls," because they were small in stature and limited in their competence.

Seeing people with intellectual disabilities as if they were little children works in tandem with the institutional attitude of "doing for." The people who live in institutional settings are seen as dependent, needy and helpless. So, like children, they are not allowed to make choices or make mistakes. Unfortunately, in our society people who are seen as children are not afforded the same rights and opportunities as adults.

People with I/DD Depicted in Childlike Imagery

An adult is determined by virtue of age and not intellect. They are not children in adult bodies.

Restriction on Choice and Decision-Making

The opportunity to make the decisions that affect our lives is one of the most cherished freedoms we have. Choices are the essence of what we consider a life of quality and opportunity—whether they are the small daily choices of what time we wish to go to bed or what we want to eat for supper, or a major life choice like what house to buy or with whom we wish to live.

Meaningful choice-making has two components, the *opportunity* to choose, and a *set of options* from which to choose. Most of us are used to having the "right" to choose for ourselves. It is part of being an adult in a country with a history and heritage of freedom. We all realize, though, that the range of things from which we can choose usually has limits. They are "bounded." We have the right to choose to drive any car we like, for example, but our options may be limited by our financial means. We have the right to choose to marry anyone we fall in love with, but our options are limited to the choice of someone who wants to marry us. Choice is an inalienable right to be free from coercion and compulsion; options are dependent on availability and the means at our disposal. Institutional settings restrict both the opportunity to choose and the options from which to make those choices. This occurs for a number of reasons.

Group size. Because of the sheer number of individuals living together, people in institutions may be severely limited in the options available for what they wear, eat, watch on TV or listen to on a radio station. All these decisions are made for the group, on the basis of the perceived needs of the group (including the staff).

Perceived danger. Because the opportunity for risk is denied or unnecessarily restricted, persons who live in institutions are prohibited from participating in many of life's activities that contain an element of danger. They do not have the option of going into town alone when they feel like "getting away." And they certainly cannot choose to experience the exhilaration of rock-climbing, water-skiing or hang-gliding.

Age appropriateness. Because people who live in institutions are frequently seen as dependent children, they are only "permitted" the kinds of options that children would be allowed. They are not seen as adults who have their own drives, dreams, desires and needs, and who may have some idea of what kinds of risk they would like to take.

Expediency. Institutions often limit options for this reason. It simply is not possible to let six hundred people all decide what they want to eat for breakfast. But, in the case of institutions for persons with intellectual disabilities or mental illness–conditions that may compromise a person's *ability to choose*–the limitations are not merely on the range of options available. Restrictions extend to the process of choice-making itself. A person with compromised cognitive functioning is often not allowed to make choices because support persons assume he does not know how to choose.

If such a person is given options, they assume, he might choose something that is "inappropriate." This might include going out into the world, with all its risks and opportunities, and breaking away from the well-meant care that is given in exchange for the loss of his freedom.

The Governor of Massachusetts expressed this concern in 1883, when he wrote, "A well-fed, well cared for idiot is a happy creature. An idiot awakened to his condition is a miserable one." The person who is not "awakened to his condition," one kept in a state of dependent ignorance, will be seen not only as lacking the *ability to choose*, but

Van Therapy

Am I cured yet?

Two more miles.

Cruising the neighborhood as a therapeutic intervention

also as not requiring a *range of options* from which to choose. The oppressor has always known this about the oppressed.

"Readiness" expectations. A person who is seen as lacking the prerequisite skills for making choices often has "choice-making" goals set for her on a Habilitation, Treatment or Education Plan. She may be required to attend "choice-making" classes in school, in which three different items are presented in clear plexiglass compartments. The "student" is then asked to "choose" which she wants. When she meets our criteria–that is, she can make the choice "with eighty percent accuracy"–she gets to move on to the next program.

But, she is not allowed to be presented with real options so she can learn to choose those things that are truly meaningful to her and substantially affect the quality of her life. For example, she cannot choose what to eat for dinner, what time to wake up on Saturday or what movie to watch. Once again, someone is required to pass a test of prerequisite skills before being allowed to try her hand at real-life situations.

The problem with this system is that people, in fact, learn to make choices by having choices to make–meaningful choices from desired options. Isn't that the way most of us live? And, yes, people with limiting conditions sometimes do make *bad* choices. They choose things that are harmful to them or too expensive, or actions that impinge on the rights of others. Just like Us.

The difference is that we have the opportunity to learn about the consequences of our choice-making by making choices. If we bought the wrong car, we will soon know it. But no one has the audacity to tell us that we have to prove our ability to pick the right car *before* we are allowed to try it. Having options and making choices are treasured aspects of the freedom we value so highly. Institutions take that freedom away.

Large Group Functions

Here comes the fifteen-passenger van with the handicapped license plates, high-domed roof, and sign across the side that declares "Specialized Vocational Services." As it pulls into the parking lot at the municipal park, the Normatives who are lunching in the picnic area tense up with concern. When the group of awkward-looking folks enters the area, the well-meaning citizens offer their tables.

"No, it's all right. You all probably want to sit together. We'll just go over to this other area."

So, the people from "the workshop" are left Outside with "their own kind" again, and they lose another opportunity for the relationships that come from participation in the events of community life.

Large group functions are the norm in an institution. They are the result of expediency. Large group functions are not a strategy applied by the staff to achieve the institution's purpose. Rather, there is only one van, a limited number of staff and only so much time in which to eat.

Recreation and leisure opportunities are limited, so they cannot be wasted on a single individual. Instead, everybody does whatever the scheduled activity for the evening is. And, thus, everybody in the community flees (emotionally as well as physically) from the onslaught at the park. The mother in the park will not approach a "deviant group," but she might talk to the shy-looking woman who seems to want to push the merry-go-round.

The other bowlers will let the "deviant group" have its own lanes, and they will never see what a friendly guy the man is who wears the helmet.

Mall Herding

The restaurant manager will offer the "deviant group" their own private dining area, and Sally will never have the chance to see and hear how people outside her group eat together at Denny's.

This is one institutional characteristic that happens very often in community-based living situations that proclaim they are not institutions. It happens when creative solutions are not found for the ever-present staff and budget shortages (only two staff, only one van, only ninety minutes until "shift change," only two dollars per week in the activity fund, and so on).

In such instances, the expediency of agency concerns overrides the need for a person to have individual opportunities for meeting and interacting with others in his or her community. Large group activities happen when staff are insensitive to the social consequences of not assisting a person to have this kind of meaningful, one-to-one contact with people in their towns and neighborhoods.

TALE
Two Group Homes – 6 a.m.

I had the opportunity to visit two group homes on two mornings at six a.m. Now, six a.m. is the Achilles' heel of congregate living situations. Some of the staff who are working have been up all night and are getting to the end of their working period.

Others have just arrived at work, perhaps having skipped that second cup of coffee. The people living there, who are just waking up to start the day, may or may not be "morning people."

There is a lot to get done because people are getting ready for work or school, and have limited time in which to do everything. Six in the morning is a time when creeping institutionalism can rear its ugly head, revealing a tendency to do things the easiest way, the "do for" way.

In the first home I visited, a home for persons who have significant intellectual disabilities, a staff person was walking down the hall, flinging the bedroom doors open and calling into each room, "Time to get

> **Hands in Pocket Training**
>
>
>
> - Be a quiet voice of support in the distance.
> - Do not nurture, cue or prompt dependence.

up!" She then returned to the kitchen, where she was cooking a big pot of oatmeal and a large skillet of scrambled eggs.

Another staff person was going from room to room, laying out clothes for the day. She gave another prompt to those still sleeping, "C'mon, time to get up." When all the clothes were laid out, the same staff person made the rounds of the bedrooms again, this time herding recalcitrant residents to the bathroom for their turn at the wipe face–brush teeth–comb hair routine. It was a very efficient assembly line for the completion of the group's morning hygiene tasks.

As soon as each resident was finished with the face wipe, he or she would shuffle to the dining room table and sit at a place that was set with bowl, plate and spoon. The kitchen staff person then came around with the oatmeal and eggs, spooning a quantity into each plate and bowl. When everyone was finished eating (except Doris, who did not eat because she wanted an English muffin, and it was not on the menu), cups were handed out. The staff person came around with the coffee carafe and poured one cup of decaf into each person's cup. The coffee was drunk in a gulp.

Then the command was given to, "Get your coats and get in the van." The whole herd shuffled out to the van, and the workday began.

A few blocks away, on the following morning, I visited another group home, very similar to the first–same 6 a.m., same six bedrooms, same kitchen and same significant intellectual disabilities. When I entered the home, it was so quiet I wondered if anyone was there. A staff person was standing with her ear to a bedroom door.

"What are you doing?" I asked.

"I'm listening for Tom's alarm clock to go off," she replied. "We help him set it every evening. In the morning when it rings, I give him a few minutes to get up on his own. If I don't hear him, I'll go in and give him a little reminder."

Soon, we heard alarm clocks buzzing all up and down the hall. We saw some people in pajamas walking purposefully back and forth between their bedrooms and the bathroom. Each person took care of his or her morning hygiene needs (with needed support and assistance supplied in a very unobtrusive way by staff). Each person left the bathroom to the next person, who was likely occupying the waiting time by making his bed. The staff person moved quietly through the area, giving each person any support that was needed.

Meanwhile, in the kitchen, three residents were intently focused on preparing their own breakfasts. Scott had just removed his toast from the toaster and was calmly spreading peanut butter and tartar sauce (his favorite breakfast combo) in just the right amounts.

Eva was next at the toaster. She had been asked to get her waffles out of the freezer, and she stood trying to unwrap some frozen hamburger patties. The staff person (the kitchen assistant) helped Eva put the patties away, find the waffles, and get them into the toaster.

Joe was making his sandwich to take to work. When he was finished, he put on his coat and poured himself another cup of coffee. He was careful to get his coffee from the pot marked "Regular." He showed us the two pots, made a face and said, "Decaf, no way."

Joe then went out to the patio to get a breath of fresh air and drink another cup of coffee before time to leave. While there, he noticed the bird feeder needed to be filled, so he went back into the house and got some sunflower seeds.

Helen got her coffee (decaf) and took it into the living room where she always watched a few minutes of "Good Morning, America." She said she did not like to eat breakfast, so she took a sweet roll with her for the first morning break at the workshop.

When everyone started to get on the van, they each came up to us to say goodbye. Scott asked me to come back again sometime and have supper. I said I would love to, and wished everyone a good day at work.

I had been at two different "facilities" at a difficult time of the day. At one, I found many of the characteristics of an institution—people participating in staff schedules. At the other, I found people living together with decency, respect and independence—staff participating in people's morning routines. One group was getting the morning routine done; the other was assisting people to start another productive day in their lives.

It should be clear by now what is meant by the adage "An institution is not a place; it is a state of mind." It means that any place can become an institution if it has the characteristics of an institution. How many characteristics of the institution are there? How many ways

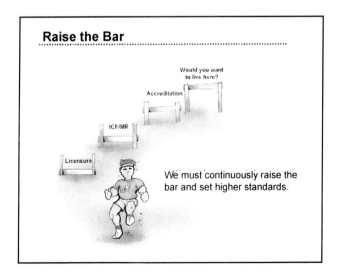

Raise the Bar

We must continuously raise the bar and set higher standards.

can you make someone's life miserable? They are limitless. This has merely been a review of some of those characteristics.

We need to keep those institutional characteristics foremost in our consciousness for the same reason we need to keep reminding ourselves of the mind states that led to the Holocaust in Nazi Germany. We can ill afford to say, "It can't happen here," whether we are talking about a big, state-run facility, a little family care home, or a small apartment where one man with significant disabilities receives support. If we fail to attend to the Quality of Life and are beguiled and distracted by the superficial appearance of the residence, we will be unable to fight creeping institutionalization wherever it is manifest.

Though the past few decades have indeed brought progress, we should not smile and pat ourselves on the backs for the "deinstitutionalization" that has greatly reduced the population of this country's large, state-run care facilities. We have no reason to be proud, especially if the people who once lived there now live a life degraded by the characteristics of the institution, whether in an apartment they call their own or in a group home with five other people.

We are afraid that there may be an untold number of little institutions scattered throughout every community, in your neighborhood and ours. We must activate our "institutional characteristics eyes" and keep our vigilance high.

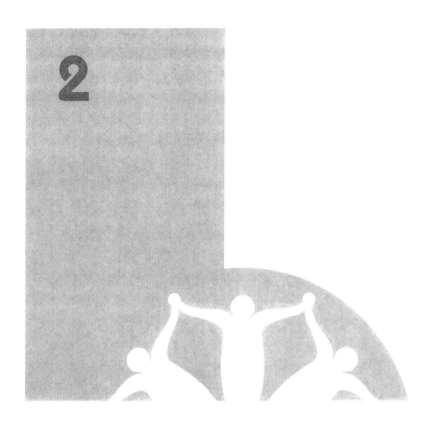

Challenging the Gatekeepers

Only Barrels Have Capacities: The Developmental Model

The Medical/Custodial Model of care, as outlined in the previous section, held sway in large, state-funded institutions as well as community agencies for many decades. But, there were always people who believed there was another way–a better way. Indeed, the name of the service model devised by Dr. Marc Gold in the early 1960s was "Try Another Way." Dr. Gold wrote, "The mentally retarded person is characterized by the level of power needed in the training process required for him or her to learn, and not by limitations in what he or she can learn." He was acknowledging the fact that a person's disabilities would remain, but that we had the power to help him or her overcome limitations.

This concept of "the level of power needed" is crucial to understanding the new service model that began to take hold in service delivery systems for people with intellectual disabilities in the 1960s and 1970s–the Developmental Model. Under this new model, we acknowledged the fact that people learn in varied ways and at different rates. We began to understand more about a person's rate of learning. The final extent of the competence/knowledge that people can gain, their "development," is determined not by the presence of brain lesions or chromosomal anomalies (medical disability) but, more importantly, by the technology and resources we are prepared to use in providing supports and assistance (overcoming disabilities).

This view that success is limited, not by the personal characteristics of the Outsider but by our willingness to remove barriers and offer creatively conceived supports, was a giant step toward Universal Enhancement. In Marc Gold's seminal notions, we find the seeds of our proposal: all conditions or attributes perceived as limiting (skin color, sexual orientation, religious conviction, contagious disease, subnormal intellectual functioning) can be transcended, if the society is willing to remove from the backs of Outsiders the stigmas and burdens they have been forced to carry.

Another intellectual current that led to the formulation of the Developmental Model was the articulation of the concept of "child development" by psychologists Jean Piaget, Erik Erikson and others. Child development theorists observed children as they grew, and reached the conclusion that maturation from childhood to adulthood was an orderly process that follows a step-wise course from one skill to another.

For example, most children learn to crawl before they learn to walk, and they can build a tower with three blocks before they can make one with five. Child development was seen as a building process, each new skill resting on the foundation laid by those abilities that were acquired earlier. The foundation was a prerequisite for subsequent steps.

Definitions

- Disability: A pathology of the individual
  - Cataracts
  - Arthritis
  - Cerebral Palsy
  - Asthma

- Handicap: Resultant impairment in performance
  - Unable to see objects at a distance
  - Unable to negotiate stairs
  - Unable to close doors
  - Unable to grasp objects with hand

It was not long before professionals working with people with intellectual disabilities began to envision the application of child development theories to their work. Soon, an intellectual disability was seen, not as an incurable disease but as a "developmental" disability, wherein some people plateaued in the developmental process and were thus unable to proceed to "higher" steps. The child who had not yet learned to say "Mama" could certainly not say, "Drink of water, please."

Following Gold's challenge to develop new technologies and methods, the first task for professionals working with a person with intellectual disabilities became clear. They would identify, through assessment, the levels of performance the subject demonstrated in various skill areas (domains). After the assessment process would come the instructional process, in which the skills believed to be prerequisite for movement to the next level of development are taught.

Systematizing Development

In order to organize and systematize this movement from assessment to instruction, a vast array of *developmental data documents* (DDDs) were developed and aggressively marketed. These documents organized normal development into domains or skill areas, such as *fine motor, gross motor, communication, socialization* and *daily living*. Then, they prescribed the normative sequence of how skills are acquired in the typical child. The trainer's job was to assess the "level" of the learner's skills in each domain, then train for movement to the next developmental step as indicated on the DDD. Formal or contrived training situations were developed with a primary focus on the person's weaknesses.

Until the person learned the skills in sequence, per the program planning profile, he was unable to move to the next step in the sequence. If he were unable or had no desire to learn the skill, he would be forever trapped in a designated chronological age grouping.

Advantages

One obvious improvement of this model over the Medical/Custodial is that it acknowledges the possibility that a person with intellectual disabilities can grow, learn and develop new abilities. Institutional staff who had previously been trained only as caretakers (*doers for*) were expected to become trainers (*doers to*). People seen as "developmentally delayed" started to attend special education classes and training programs, so that they could work on attaining the skills they should have acquired in the normal developmental evolution.

Another advantage of the Developmental Model was that the program plans for skill acquisition training were individualized, based on real assessments of the person's strengths and weaknesses. It made an honest attempt to treat people as individuals and to help them acquire the skills and competencies the developmental assessments identified as lacking.

Finally, the structured nature of this model permitted a somewhat objective and standardized evaluation of the effectiveness of programming. Program evaluators could see who was making progress. In addition, they could assess the effectiveness of overall programs by comparing them to standardized DDDs.

This new paradigm was celebrated because it reduced the emphasis on the severity of a person's disability. And, it increased the importance of finding creative ways to help people overcome the limitations that challenged them. If we criticize the Developmental Model now, it is only through 20/20 hindsight. Elements of developmental awareness and emphasis survive in the new definitions of intellectual disabilities because of the stress on the amount and kind of supports and services a person needs, rather than some purported description of a person's inherent lack of ability.

Problems: Age Equivalents

There were problems, of course. Frequently, a major difficulty arose from the fact that the norms used to assess where on the developmental scale a person's abilities fell were taken from the typical developmental sequence, as observed in children. Thus, people with very elementary abilities were frequently compared to young children who had similar abilities.

This comparison gave rise to the notion of "age equivalents." Jack, age forty, lacked the skill to tie his shoes and could only talk in two- or three-word sentences. He might be said to perform at a level equivalent to that of a child who was thirty months old. This evaluation nurtured the demeaning notion that people with intellectual disabilities are really just "children in adult bodies."

In order to get Jack's test score up to his normative age equivalent, it would be necessary to train him to demonstrate all the skills the typical person learns from ages two to forty. But, as we get to know him better, we see that Jack knows how to do a lot of things never dreamed of by the average two-year-old. Some of the words in those two- or three-word utterances are ones that Billy the toddler has never heard. And, Jack can use a match to light his cigarette, a fairly complex fine motor task, even though he is unable to make a stack of five blocks.

We find that people with intellectual disabilities learn a variety of things that are scattered all over the developmental hierarchy. We call these abilities "splinter skills" because they are fragments broken off of the main course of development.

Upon closer inspection of these splinter skills, we see something that leads us to a remarkable conclusion. We suddenly realize that these "extra" abilities people have learned are the skills that are important to them, that help them obtain the objects, events and relationships that make their lives worthwhile. No adult has "the mind of a child." There is much more that comprises a person's mind or personality than demonstrated competence and ability. Basing the age equivalent of a person solely on functional skills, as specified in a DDD, ignores a whole range of attitudes, desires, urges, compulsions, and relationships that influence and form who and what a person is.

MAXIM: *An adult is determined by virtue of age, not intellect.* ™

Likewise, learning the next logical step in a predetermined sequence of development does not assure the enhancement of the person's Quality of Life. That step on the psychologist's chart may not be reflective of what is really important to that person. We say metaphorically, "Underarm deodorant is not where it's at," because people who are subjected to endless training programs to learn to put on underarm deodorant may not be working on achieving outcomes that are truly valuable to them.

Yes, "Applies underarm deodorant" may be the next skill on the developmental checklist, but it may occupy no spot at all on this person's list of life goals, nor contribute in any way to his or her Quality of Life.

TALE

Flowers Are Not in Your IEP, Young Man
by Gary J. Makuch

"Teacher," the young man said, "I found this flower over the weekend, and I want to know what made it grow."

"Look, young man, you're in special education. You must have an IEP. It's the law, you see. And flowers are not in your IEP, young man! You have short term objectives in math and reading, young man. You have long range goals in self-help and getting along with others. But flowers are not in your IEP, young man!"

"But, teacher," the young man said, "I really want to know what makes the flowers grow."

"Look, young man, your mother and father and the principal and I wrote your IEP, and then we signed it. That's the law, you see. And flowers are not in your IEP, young man!

"Your IEP has an evaluation component, young man. It's the law, you see. And I want you to reach your objectives and attain your goals. There's no time for anything else, and besides...flowers are not in your IEP, young man!"

"Please, teacher," the young man said. "I'd rather learn about flowers than math or reading."

"Okay, young man, if you insist, but this will be a significant change in your IEP and your parents will have to agree. It's the law, you see."

A month later...

"A conference was held, the IEP was revised, procedural safeguards were observed and all the necessary paperwork completed. It's the law, you see.

"And flowers are now in your IEP, young man."

"But, teacher," the young man said, "my flower is dead, and I found a frog over the weekend and now I want to know what made it grow."

"Look, young man, your mother and father and the principal met and revised your IEP, and then we signed it. That's the law, you see. And flowers are now in your IEP.

"You have short term objectives in math, reading, and flowers, young man. You have long range goals in self help and getting along with others.

"But frogs are not in your IEP, young man!"

Problems: Getting Stuck

The second problem with the Developmental Model is similar to the first. If the mission is to train a person only in the lowest level of skills not demonstrated on the developmental chart, the trainee may become stuck there and never go on to any "higher level" skills. If "completing a twenty-piece puzzle" is a prerequisite to "playing a simple card game," our friend Jack could be stuck doing his Puzzle Program until doomsday and might never have the opportunity to play a rousing game of UNO with his buddies.

When the Developmental Model was dominant, it filtered our perception. Locked into the notion that certain skills were prerequisites for learning more "advanced" tasks, we had people working on endless "pre-language" programs and "pre-vocational" programs and "pre-leisure" programs. They were stuck at the step on which they tested out, never having the opportunity to use the skills they had cobbled together in years of real-life experience. There was obviously something wrong. As Dr. Lou Brown insightfully noted, "pre" must actually mean "never," because the people we were working with never seemed to get on to the next step of the training program, let alone the real business of living.

The Developmental Model is a "readiness" model of service. It seeks to prepare a person for the next developmental step, training program, job placement or residential alternative. When the person being trained passes the test, demonstrating mastery of all the prerequisite skills deemed necessary, she is granted permission to enter the environment in which those skills can be exercised. The Gatekeepers have determined that she has achieved the "right" of passage.

Thus, getting a person ready to move on to something else is still performing a "do to" form of service. We professionals are in the driver's seat, deciding what teaching tasks are presented when, and meting out access to opportunity based on our tests. We are blind to the fact that, when provided with the appropriate supports, a person will generally learn the skills she needs for engaging in the activities that are available and valuable to her.

```
The To's
─────────────────────────────

To Care For    To Do For     Sympathy

To Do To       To Program    Manage

To Do With     To Care About Empathy
```

Problems: Discipline Boundaries

This brings us to a third problem with the Developmental Model. It tends to support an *intra*-disciplinary model for those professionals who subscribe to its tenets and apply its principles. That is to say, each professional has a clinical specialization in one of the domains assessed by the DDD. This "professional bag of tricks" relates to only one aspect of a person, not to the whole.

For example, if I am a speech pathologist, I test Lucy with a device that determines the normalized age equivalent for Lucy's current communication skills. I then devise a training program (or apply one that has been developed specifically to be keyed to the testing device) to help Lucy work her way up through the developmental progression of normal language acquisition. I may determine from her test scores that she needs to learn noun-verb sequencing, so I will schedule two weekly sessions where Lucy will manipulate symbol tiles for subjects and objects.

I may know that Lucy tells the "direct care" staff she wants a Coke by repeatedly tapping her lips with two fingers. But, my commitment to moving Lucy through the steps of normative language development blinds me to the importance of this functional communication. I see Lucy's attempts at communicating her wants and needs as "splinter skills." If I believe in the Developmental Model, I believe that Lucy cannot engage in meaningful, functional communication until she has the prerequisite skills. My job is to address Lucy's language acquisition, and I need not concern myself with other areas of her life.

When you multiply this narrow, one-discipline concern times all of the disciplines involved in Lucy's training (*cognitive skills, self-care, activities of daily living, socialization, recreation/leisure*), Lucy's day becomes driven by a compartmentalized master schedule. At pre-scheduled times, Lucy is transported all around "campus," receiving training from competent professionals on various skill deficits that

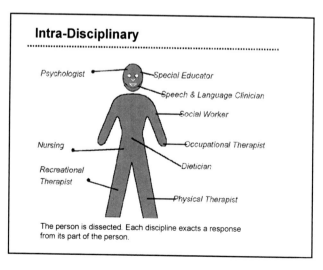

The person is dissected. Each discipline exacts a response from its part of the person.

have been determined by validated testing devices. Progress notes submitted by each discipline indicate that Lucy is slowly advancing up the developmental ladder (so slowly that her skill level will never catch up with her ever-advancing chronological age).

The tragedy is that an enormous amount of time and energy are spent on Lucy's assessment, training and documentation, all with very little development of Lucy's communication skills. In reality, the people attending to Lucy's real day-to-day needs are not the discipline-bound professionals, but rather those who work directly with her, those who are building *relationships* with her.

Problems: Only Barrels Have Capacities

Finally, another problem with the Developmental Model is that it reinforces the notion of capacity. People are shown, through test results, to have the capacity to reach particular milestones, but go no further.

Now, if someone asked you, "Have you reached your capacity?" you would probably have a difficult time answering the question. You might even have a hard time understanding what the person was asking. Typically, we do not think of ourselves as having inherent limitations, a capacity beyond which we can never progress. More likely, we think of ourselves as always growing and developing.

MAXIM: *Only barrels have capacities–not human beings.*

Historically, many professionals, and subsequently, society at large, have not hesitated to apply the concept of capacity to people who have disabilities. Someone might say, "He has the capacity of a three-year-old" or "She has reached her capacity." The notion of a capacity that cannot be exceeded is like a barrel that will only hold so much. A five-gallon barrel will hold anything up to five gallons, but never seven gallons. Likewise, a person who is seen as having the capacity of a toddler will never learn the skills needed by an adult.

The belief that a person has a limited capacity becomes a self-fulfilling prophecy. We who support persons with intellectual disabilities

 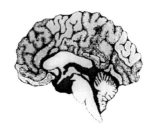

Only barrels have capacities... not the human mind.

never try to teach people skills that we do not believe they are capable of learning. This is essential to decisions regarding support and assistance. If we believe the limits to learning and cognitive growth are that person's rather than ours (and we reinforce our belief with validated test results), that person will never go beyond the limits we impose.

When we see limited capacities, we offer limited opportunities, and limited effort and resources. This narrow view perpetuates a

Think Outside the Box

Supporting others in realizing their preferred futures is a creative process.

learned helplessness so we can continue in our efforts to do for. Shame on us.

A basic tenet of Gold's "better way" says that people stop growing, developing and learning new skills not because they have reached their limits but because we have reached the limits of our technology, resources and skills. Only when we are willing to divest ourselves of the destructive notion of capacity as it applies to human beings will we be able to enhance everyone's lives, including our own.

TALE
An End to the Concept of Handicapped– Oh, What a Beautiful Mourning
by Marc W. Gold

If you could only know me for who I am
Instead of for who I am not
There would be so much more to see
'Cause there's so much more that I've got.

So long as you see me as handicapped,
Which supposedly means something, I guess,
There is nothing that you or I could ever do
To make me a human success.

Someday you'll know that tests aren't built
To let me stand next to you.
By the way you test me, all they can do
Is make me look bad through and through.

And someday soon I'll get my chance,
When some of you finally adapt.
You'll be delighted to know that though
I'm disabled, I'm not at all handicapped.

5

Gatekeepers and Other Exclusionists: The Habilitation Model

In Section One, when the notion was discussed that there are three groups of people–Insiders, Us and Outsiders–the concept of the Gatekeeper was introduced. The Gatekeeper is the person or organization that decides who is an Insider, who is Us, and who is cast outside. Society at large has generally empowered professionals of various stripes to be "Gatekeepers of record," the arbiters of inclusion and exclusion. The gate that keeps people out of the coveted insider realm is often controlled by critics and intellectuals, those who are deemed to be "informed" when it comes to who should be honored and revered. And, though we appoint professionals to articulate the justification for guarding the gate that separates Us from the Outsiders, the real criteria are usually based on ignorance, prejudice and fear.

Which profession gets to make and justify decisions about who gets to pass which gate varies according to the relevant filter, or basis, for accepting or rejecting people. For example, where people are excluded on the basis of not having the correct religious beliefs, clergymen are the Gatekeepers. When people are excluded on the basis of criminal activity, courts and judges take on the role. Where sanity is the test, psychiatrists are the Gatekeepers.

THE GATEKEEPER

In the Medical/Custodial Model, physicians were the Gatekeepers. The solemn, educated, professional person in the white coat had the authority to look at a child with Down syndrome and tell her parents, "I'm sorry, Mr. and Mrs. Smith. Susie will always have the mind of a child. She will never learn anything and will have to be put in an institution." The parents, heartbroken, would prepare themselves for the inevitable. The Gatekeeper had spoken. Later, the same Gatekeeper physician could tell Mr. Smith's son, "I'm sorry. Your father has advanced Alzheimer's disease. He will have to be placed in a nursing home."

In the Developmental Model, the developmental psychologist or special educator became the Gatekeeper. They designed and administered DDDs that assigned people a life circumstance according to "age equivalent." For instance: "This young man," quoth the Gatekeeper, "has the full scale equivalent functioning level of a typical person of the age of four years, three months. He will be best served in a preschool type of environment."

The Habilitation Model is grounded in the belief that the acquisition of skills is what allows a person to pass the Gatekeeper and enter into a "less restrictive environment" (LRE), a mythical place that is seen as the true goal for all people who have disabilities or other Outsider conditions. Of course, "less restrictive environment" is not a specific geographical place. Any place becomes a less restrictive environment when restrictions are lifted. You cannot get to the LRE by plane or bus, but you do need a ticket. The ticket to passage is the acquisition of those skills the Gatekeepers require for you to be stamped "Okay."

For example, Tommy, age twenty-eight, wears protective undergarments because he does not use the toilet independently. He lives in a large, state-operated residence because none of the community-based service providers will accept him in diapers. Officials of Tommy's residential facility have determined that Tommy needs to be taught to eliminate reliably in the toilet, so that he can move out of his current residence into a less restrictive residential setting. He needs to be habilitated. He will not have the opportunity to get a real life until he passes the test for appropriate toileting behavior.

Habilitation is the process of preparing someone for such a test. We drill and rehearse them until they are ready to pass. Indeed, the word habilitate means "to impart an ability or capacity to; to qualify." It comes from the Latin *habilitate*, which means, "to enable" (*The American Heritage Dictionary*). Thus, habilitation is the acquisition of those abilities that enable one to qualify for full acceptance in the

Untouchables

The inappropriate use of rubber gloves proclaims that others are of the caste of the untouchables.

community at large. Under this model, you must meet arbitrary requirements of competence in order to be allowed to have a life.

The Gatekeepers of the Habilitation Model believe it is a person's lack of skill that imposes restrictions and limitations on life circumstances and opportunities in which he or she can be "permitted" to participate. In this model, a wide variety of service providers and community agencies serve as Gatekeepers. Social workers, psychologists, eligibility specialists, vocational rehabilitators, and a host of other arbiters judge people on the basis of their demonstrating or not demonstrating the skills deemed necessary for them to move from restrictive, isolating "placements" to freer, less restrictive, less assistive environments.

The Habilitation Model is frequently managed through an *interdisciplinary team* that performs assessments and evaluations aimed at identifying the "required skill" deficits. The staff of the habilitation program then set about to facilitate the person's acquisition of those skills. They help the person meet the standards and procure his ticket to ride. The Habilitation Model is certainly more progress-oriented than the Medical/Custodial Model, and it is more sensitive and practical than the Developmental Model. Indeed, it is a plausible way to serve people who live in environments with institutional characteristics. It is the core philosophy of many regulatory and funding agencies, such as the Intermediate Care Facility-Mental Retardation (ICF-MR) Regulations. These rules govern many residential service providers that receive funding under Title XIX of the Medicaid program.

Systems and Standards

Based on regulatory and funding agency expectations, then, organizations providing services to people with intellectual disabilities have typically used the Habilitation Model as a foundation. In this review of the historically-predominant regulatory standards for services for persons with intellectual disabilities, the reader may substitute a review of the regulations and standards from his or her own field. The Habilitation Model and its principles can be found in any service provision system that sees skill acquisition—whether it be the ability to

move the wheels of your wheelchair, stay away from alcohol, or refrain from responding to voices that only you hear—as the ticket to a life free from restrictions imposed by well-meaning assistance.

At the heart of the model of service that Title XIX mandates are the Individualized Habilitation Plan (IHP) and the Interdisciplinary Team. The team is composed mainly of people from the disciplines that have historically provided services to people with disabilities. These include psychology; social work; nursing; physical, occupational and communication therapy; and others like them. Representatives from each of the disciplines conduct assessments and formal evaluations of the person. They take an *intra*-disciplinary approach; that is, they limit the scope and view to the ones imposed by their disciplines. Next, a representative of each discipline participates in an Interdisciplinary Team meeting to discuss the person's current strengths, needs and recommendations for programming for the next year.

The head of the team, designated by various titles (QMHP, QDDP, training coordinator, program director, or other designation, depending on the agency), assembles all of the recommendations. She also records the substance of the team discussion and formulates annual goals for the "client." The "client" is required to attend the team meeting where deemed appropriate. But, in reality, an attitude

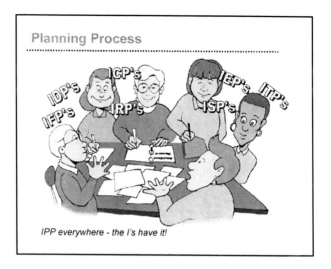

IPP everywhere - the I's have it!

often prevails among the professionals that they know what is best for the person who is the subject of the planning. If that person is legally incompetent or a minor, the team encourages a guardian or parent to attend the meeting and approve the plan. The completed IHP then becomes the controlling document for service provision and progress evaluation for the next service year.

A similar process is used in the pubic schools under the mandates of Public Law 94-142, The Right to Education of All Handicapped Children Act of 1975. The document that results is called an Individualized Education Plan (IEP). And, similar processes are currently used for a wide variety of disenfranchised persons, whether the resulting document is the Individualized Treatment Plan for persons with psychiatric disorders, the Plan of Care for elderly persons in nursing homes, or the Aftercare Plan for people recovering from addiction. Although the programs operate under the guise of a support program, the main focus is a habilitation outcome.

Doing "To"

The Habilitation Model for service delivery is always a "do to" model. People who are experts in the field identify a person's needs, limitations and skill deficits for the purpose of setting goals for him or her. Other experts then conduct formal training or therapy programs designed to give the person the skills he or she needs for a move to a less restrictive "placement." Whatever the condition being treated, it is the training protocols, methodologies and documentation that assume paramount importance, with skill acquisition being the result. In this model, *the process of habilitation* is, in fact, the goal. The standard for measuring progress is success in meeting program goals. More independence and a higher Quality of Life are merely fortuitous.

MAXIM: *Habilitation is not a goal; it is a result.* ™

In subsequent chapters, this last assertion will be turned on its head. Its proponents maintain that habilitation and skill acquisition come about as a result of community participation, rather than as goals in and of themselves to be pursued as prerequisites to getting permission to access one's community.

In order to better understand how habilitation serves as an exclusionary obstacle, let us take a deeper look at some of the pros and cons of the Habilitation Model. This is necessary because habilitation is the principle service paradigm of most publicly funded residential programs for people who have some sort of excluding disability.

Some Steps in the Right Direction
Though habilitation is a "do to" model, it does, when implemented at its best, have elements that point toward the kind of collaborative endeavor we advocate in Universal Enhancement. A team works together in an interdisciplinary fashion to assess a person's strengths and needs, and set goals with much discussion across the parochial lines of narrow professional expertise. This approach should really become "transdisciplinary," going beyond the usual scope of professional expertise. The "client" should be approached as a whole person, with strengths that cross disciplinary lines and needs that may involve more than a simple training program strategy (unlike the Developmental Model).

Many of the features of the Habilitation Model were designed to counter some of the characteristics of an institution. Indeed, "less restrictive environment" and "deinstitutionalization" are often seen as describing the same thing. Many of the current state and federal standards for services to a wide variety of disenfranchised persons prescribe such things as individualized programming, the provision of privacy, opportunities for choice-making, the organization of life activities into small groups, and other changes that are good correctives for institutional problems.

Always Getting Ready

A redeeming feature of the Habilitation Model is that it acknowledges the fact that people can acquire new skills and gain greater independence. This belief is coupled, however, with the notion of "readiness." A man is not ready to live in his own apartment, for instance, until he has acquired and demonstrated all the skills deemed necessary for apartment living. This, of course, is determined by the Gatekeepers who regulate access to community participation. As professional service providers, we have established our credentials as Gatekeepers who are sanctioned to establish the criteria that must be met before a person can move to that less restrictive environment.

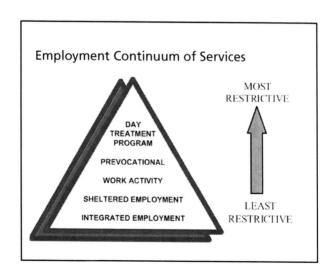

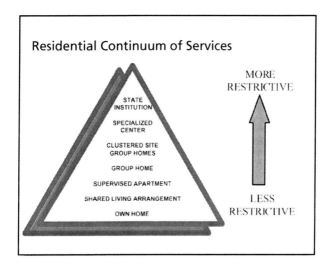

For example, we Gatekeepers are empowered to decide that Susie cannot live in an apartment of her own because she does not yet know how to "prepare simple meals that require cooking." Joe cannot live in a house with Jerry because neither of them can make a budget and plan for ordinary household expenses. Sheila cannot be left unsupervised at night because, while spending a weekend alone at her mother's house, she drank all the liquor and stayed up all night. All of these people are on training programs, devised by the Interdisciplinary Team and designed to lead to acquisition of the skills they need for the next step in independence. When motivated by the care and concern of the team members, these are laudable goals.

MAXIM: *The word "wait" is the most vulgar word in our vocabulary.* ™

The problem with imposing arbitrary prerequisite skills is that it unnecessarily and unfairly restricts (handicaps) the freedom of a person with disabilities in ways that are not imposed on most of Us. Second, it prevents the person from learning new things the way most of us acquired our knowledge–in those situations and under those conditions that supported and encouraged the application of new skills.

For example, how many young people are obliged to demonstrate cooking or budgeting skills before they are "allowed" to get their first apartment? Many of us remember learning how to heat beans and wieners, and deal with a letter from the bank telling us that our checking account was overdrawn. We learned by doing, by being immersed in and engaged with the tasks and objects of everyday life. Perhaps we called a parent or other trusted adult for advice. But, it is unlikely that we look back and regret that Mom was not there cooking for us or balancing our checkbook. In the same way, a person with disabilities is likely to want only as much assistance from others as necessary to be immersed and engaged in her preferred daily routines.

When we support a person with disabilities in this way, we say the person has *supported routines*. When a service provider makes skill acquisition a precursor to having access to the places where those tasks and objects are found, people with disabilities must live in a place with the characteristics of the institution until they are deemed ready for something else. Tragically, many people with various disabling conditions will never be able to make the grade. They will never pass the test and pass through the Gate. Too often, for them "pre-" means "never."

TALE
Try Another Way System
by Marc Gold

The person with intellectual disabilities is characterized by the level of power needed in the training process required for him or her to learn, and not by limitations in what he or she can learn.

The level of functioning of a person with an intellectual disability is determined by the availability of training technology and the amount of resources society is willing to allocate and not by significant limitations in biological potential.

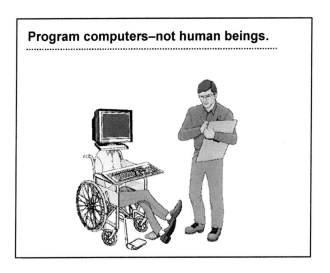

Program computers–not human beings.

Like Everyone Else

Another problem with the Habilitation Model is that it seeks to program people into acting like Normatives, conforming to some imagined standard of perfection in dress, deportment and social skills as a condition for moving to a less restrictive environment. The Interdisciplinary Team is usually quite aware of common community reactions to the various unusual behaviors and characteristics exhibited by some people who have intellectual disabilities or psychiatric disorders.

Programming goals are set for the development of "social behavior," "job-site behavior," "public transportation behavior" and "selecting appropriate clothing." The goal is to ensure that the person can blend in with others in various community settings and not stand out because of his or her deviance from the social norms.

MAXIM: *Nothing about me without me.*

Once again, this is an honorable objective, motivated by care and concern. But, more often than not, these norms and standards, the supposed keys to opening the gate to community inclusion, result in more exclusion. They serve to justify a determination of why some people can have a life and others not.

The fervent, professional desire to teach a person to conform may, unfortunately, serve as the highest obstacle of all. Most people with significant intellectual disabilities; chronic, severe mental illness; or serious physical disabilities may never look or act like typical, Normative people. They may always show such limited or impaired competency that their deviance is going to be perceived negatively. If the imposition of societal expectations requires them to "act normal" before they can be included in the community with the rest of Us, they likely will be sentenced to an institutional life.

Indeed, our institutions are currently occupied predominantly by people who will never reflect the norms of societal behavior in any conventional manner.

> **MAXIM:** *"Programming is done when you can't or won't give people a reasonable life." –Todd Risley, Ph.D.*

Universal Enhancement surmounts this obstacle, literally as if it did not exist. The new paradigm proposes that everybody has the right to be a full, participating member of his or her community without delay. There are no prerequisites. The community is not a place to which a person must gain admission. It is, rather, a condition in which people are free to make choices–life choices about where, how and with whom they would like to reside. If they are people who need supports, Universal Enhancement is the freedom to choose the form and extent of the supports, and who provides them. The ticket to freedom, the key to getting a life, is not demonstrated competence; it is opportunity.

Typically, professionals develop the schedules and routines for people to fit into versus allowing them to establish their own routines and schedules. If they do not fit into the schedule and routine, then we develop a plan to support them in fitting in. No one should have to cave in to the Competency/Deviancy Hypothesis, subjected to continual tests of competence because they are seen as deviant. People who are "different" by their very nature should be able to do their own thing and learn to brazen out the stares of Insiders and Normatives, as do men who wear earrings and women who dye their hair purple.

One meaning of the universal part of Universal Enhancement is that the benefits of Inclusion in communities accrue to both people with conditions that have caused them to be placed outside and to those without such stigmas, the Normative people. Only by advocating for integration, right now, regardless of the prejudices and ignorance of neighborhoods full of Normatives, will this mutual benefit have a chance to take root and flower.

Relationships

Finally, the Habilitation Model of providing services falls short of assuring a person real participation in life because of its emphasis. Skill acquisition, training programs, goals and objectives are seen as *ends in themselves*. This emphasis fails to embrace the importance of the development of *relationships*, the most valuable element of Quality of Life for many of us.

TALE
What If All the People in the World Were Paid to Be There?
by Bob Perske

We have only begun to sense the tragic wounds some persons with intellectual disabilities may feel when it dawns on them that the only people relating with them–outside of relatives–are paid to do so.

If you or I came to such a sad realization about ourselves, it would rip at our souls to even talk about it. Chances are some of us would cover it up with one noisy, awkward bluff after another and chances are, some professionals seeing us act this way, would say we had 'maladaptive behavior.'

Think about what it would feel like to have even one person come to us and, without pay, develop a reliable, long-term relationship with us because he or she wanted to...to literally accept us as we are. Then think of the unspeakable feelings we might possess if–when others were 'talking down' to us and 'putting us in our place'–that kind person could be counted on to defend us and stick up for us as well!

Most of us do have persons like that in our lives. But will the day ever come when citizens with intellectual disabilities will have them, too?

Relationships with others do, indeed, require skills, and many of those skills can be learned. But, they will probably not be learned in a training program. They are usually developed in situations that involve a wide variety of people with whom to relate. In the Habilitation Model, the person being trained (transformed) is prohibited from becoming part of the network of relationships we know as community *until* he or she changes–a tragic Catch-22. This intent focus on getting ready, through skill acquisition, for the big move to a less restrictive environment leaves a person little time for activities like *forming and maintaining relationships*. While they are being prepared for life, they are missing many of life's joys.

> ### Back Wards of the Community
>
> *A community characterized by:*
>
> loneliness fear anxiety discrimination
> boredom despondency pity sorrow
> hostility subjugation
> poverty indifference degradation
> isolation segregation
> rejection
> despair intimidation failure hatred
> prejudice hopelessness

Those of us who serve as that person's trainers may feel we need to use every tool at our disposal to help the person learn the necessary new skills. If we discover something the person likes, we tend to latch onto it as a "reinforcer," using it contingently to encourage appropriate behavior. We miss seeing it as a personal preference, one of the things that makes the person who she is. Everything in that person's life becomes part of a Habilitation Plan, part of therapy. As a result, she has therapeutic recreation, music therapy, pet therapy, horseback riding therapy and therapeutic conversation groups.

Likewise with relationships, professionals develop what is proudly referred to as a therapeutic relationship. The therapeutic part acknowledges that the professional is not really the person's friend or ally but stands more in the role of a therapist. Thus, we call them "clients." The professional is someone whose job it is to fix this person–a Habilitation Specialist. Or, the professional is the one charged with managing the person's case–a Case Manager. This is what the professional is trained and paid to do, and it is considered an honorable objective.

Imagine, though, how you would feel if your friends had such a condescending attitude toward you. As adults, we can barely tolerate it from our parents. We certainly would not want our friends, spouses or neighbors to act like we were a project, "a real fixer-upper" as they

> ## Being In is Not Enough
>
> - **IN** the Community   vs.   **OF** the Community
>
> | Present | Connected to |
> |---|---|
> | Located | Having a presence |
> | There | Assimilated with others |
> | | An integral part; included |
>
> - As in . . .
>   - **OF** the Jewish faith
>   - Member **OF** the Pomeranz family
>   - Member **OF** the Garden Club

say in the real estate business. Indeed, we often flee from relationships where someone is trying to straighten us out. We recognize that such relationships are unhealthy. People who are the subjects of IHPs likewise see the threat in our attempt to repair them. They push back against our plans for them. They resist working on their programs, and leave the facility premises without permission. They continue to demonstrate inappropriate social behavior that is very frustrating to us, because we know that they can do better, and we have taken their success as a mark of our professional prowess.

Generally, we have not yet stumbled on the realization that our planning, scheduling, charting and programming of people–albeit with the best of intentions–is part of the reason those same people do not make the expected progress. Our intentions are good, honorable and right, but our plans and goals may not accord with the dreams, desires and aspirations of the person receiving services. The Habilitation Model insists that we know better than They, especially if we are trained in a habilitative clinical discipline. It gives us the right, indeed the responsibility, to influence and direct important life decisions for Them. It is a cruel irony that by limiting a person's autonomy in the interest of habilitation, the person may be deprived of the most important set of opportunities everyone needs for fruitful living–self-direction, self-determination, freedom and choice.

Universal Enhancement demands that our sole role as service and support providers should be to furnish temporary assistance to the persons we serve while they develop natural supports in their community the same way we all do, through forming relationships. If we feel we need to adopt a clinical role, it should be to function as social workers, people who help people find what they need in their community, until we can literally work ourselves out of a job.

We must recognize that the community is not a distinct place that you can move to. Community is a web of relationships that we wrap around ourselves every time we interact with people in our daily lives. The community cannot be found; it must be created.

MAXIM: *The community is not there to find–it has to be built.* –John O'Brien

---

6

Learning Through Participation

People who have worked in the field of providing services to people with intellectual disabilities have been fairly well indoctrinated with the notion that the job is to "teach" people. We have subscribed to the commonly-held behaviorist notion that learning occurs as a pattern of responses to a system of rewards. Under the influence of this Learning Theory approach to skill acquisition, we see ourselves as being in possession of some valued ability, knowledge, or skill that is absent in the people we have targeted for teaching. We are like surgeons, trying to effect an "information transplant." We establish goals, objectives and training strategies to discharge our responsibilities as teachers.

This task of "fixing" a person's defects through education and training tends to shape the relationships we form with the people we are supposed to train. Perceiving ourselves as having the responsibility to "do to" someone else, puts us, the professionals, in the driver's seat. We, as the drivers, determine the destination and choose the road to be traveled. We, as teachers, decide what should be learned and how. The "student" is expected to be the welcoming and appreciative recipient of our endeavors.

If you attended the typical public school, you are all too familiar with this model. The teacher stood up front, injecting us poor students with wisdom. Many students rebelled against this traditional school system. The kind of restless dissatisfaction we felt with the notion that "the teacher knows best" is indicative of our gut reaction toward such contrived educational settings, toward being told what, when and how to learn. In fact, there is something so artificial about this kind of teacher/student relationship that many of us are drawn to ask whether this is the most desirable or effective way for people to learn. As parents, many of us have come to wonder whether our children fail because the goals and methodologies of their educational time are not relevant to improving the quality of their lives.

One alternative is an educational vision in which children participate in the processes of learning, rather than being merely passive receptacles for what someone else thinks is important information. Such a vision of participative education is a response to our growing understanding that all human beings learn in a marvelous multi-channel way. Inputs are processed at various levels, and memories are stored in great holographic hodge-podges of connections.

The active, questing two- or three-year-old is a little sponge walking through her environment soaking up information from visions and sounds and vestibular changes. She is not so much in need of a "teacher" as "opportunities to learn." She needs a rich milieu of events from which to build her internal connections. And, we tolerate a wide latitude of deviancy and variance while she is learning. We do not expect her to behave like an adult (if we have some parenting skills), and we do not try to "teach" her adult-level skills. We let her roam, ramble and soak up what she needs. Her learning is experiential.

This vision of explorative and participatory education is being implemented with typical children in many innovative school settings. By contrast, it is seldom applied to those children and adults who have disabilities. Often, their exploration "opportunities" are just difficult and tedious tasks.

"Special" Education

Let us consider, however, the possibility that our reactions to the dead hand of rote learning are not relevant to meeting the "special needs" of people with intellectual disabilities or other disabilities. Maybe there is some unique and different way people with such disabilities learn.

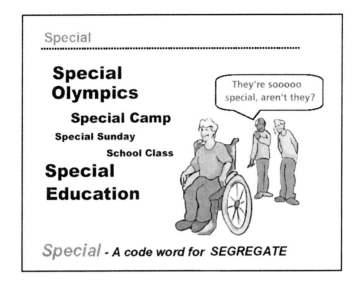

Maybe people with intellectual disabilities, mental illness or physical disabilities, with their altered cognitive and sensory abilities, are more like the rats and pigeons of the Learning Theory lab than are Normative children. If this were so, one may conclude that even if the Behaviorist Learning Theory falls through in typical schools and households with our own children, it still might have some application to those who occupy the wrong side of the Gate of Exclusion.

This proposal is false. The notion that people with disabilities and other isolating conditions are somehow essentially different from other people and therefore need "special" programs is insidious. It serves only to deny many people the opportunity to learn by participating in life with the rest of us.

The usual professional approach to people considered in need of special educational services generally gives little acknowledgment or support to the holographic, multi-channel learning style we see in our own two-year-olds. A person with disabilities is more often seen as a programmable organism that learns in some qualitatively different way from the rest of humanity. The assumption is that if They could learn things the way the rest of us do, They would have already learned those things. After all, most people who are age twenty-eight can talk.

Bob never learned to talk. Therefore, Bob must have a diminished "capacity" to learn. He must learn more like a laboratory pigeon than like a Normative his own age.

Once again, the words and language we use shape our perception. Public schools have established large, complex departments of Special Education for children who are deemed unable to learn in the conventional way. Special educators, historically, have referred to their students as being "trainable" or "educable" (one group receives training and the other education). Sometimes, children are further categorized into "multi-handicapped," "learning disabled," "behaviorally and emotionally handicapped," "sensory impaired," "culturally deprived," "attention deficit disordered," and on and on. But, this kind of categorization fails to facilitate the learning process.

Instead of labeling, which serves to separate and exclude, Universal Enhancement recognizes that all people learn in different ways, and that we *all* require special education. Everyone needs opportunities to find out who he or she is and acquire the skills, competencies or supports that enhance the quality of his or her life. We do not need to be taught, so much as we need opportunities to learn. A person with intellectual disabilities, and any other Outsider, needs nothing less.

Universal Enhancement Mentor

Universal Enhancement Mentor uses his/her experiences to help others learn and grow. You do this by listening to what a person has to say, identifying emotions which the person is not able to, and offering advice/counsel.

The ability to relate to the person's problem by telling a story helps to validate that you do understand. As an "Advisor/Counselor", you assist the individual in making life choices (without judging) which will enhance his/her life and the lives of those people around him/her.

MAXIM: *"Special" is a code word for segregation.* ™

Read biographies of accomplished individuals as well as common folk, and note how often you encounter a description of a significant event that a young person experienced. Maybe it was a time when a neighbor took a young violinist to a concert, a grandfather shared the rudiments of gardening, or a kindly librarian opened up the world of books. People who have achieved real life gains, people who have caught hold of life's shiny brass rings, have not had knowledge and ability poured into them from a pitcher as if they were empty glasses. Their Quality of Life was enhanced by being exposed to opportunities that caused them to develop new skills and occasions that allowed them to apply solutions in the company of caring supporters.

We need to fulfill the role of Caring Supporter for the person who has been cast aside. A caring ally coaches and supports the person through the difficult tasks and challenges he encounters in the world. Unfortunately, this assignment is not consistent with the conventional image of the teacher. We must give up the control aspects of the teacher "doing to" the passively receiving student and begin to relate to the people to whom we provide supports as our peers and equals. In this process, we begin to be open to the reality that the need for supports and assistance is universal. We are all interdependent members of the fabric of relationships we call community.

Responsive Learning

One of the objections that should be raised to being teachers instead of coaches or guides is that the classic teaching model assumes that there is a right curriculum (from the Latin word for racetrack, a place for running around in circles). The curriculum is a template that the learner has to match or fit. In all the major Learning Theory models, the teacher (or the principal or curriculum committee) is seen as the master of the template, the person who sets the standards. The student's job is to learn how to fit the mold.

Universal Enhancement Ally

Universal Enhancement Ally is a person who will do whatever he/she can to help others in their endeavors. He/She acts as a support during difficult times and reaffirms a commitment to assist in any way possible, until the troubled times have passed.

Very few, if any, people can go through life without the support and encouragement of those closest to them. We should strive, therefore, to always see ourselves in the role of Ally; helping those we support to see us as people they can depend upon to help them through difficult times and become as independent as possible.

A review of some of the models of service provision for persons with intellectual disabilities indicates that this is a common problem. The standards–required tasks and hoops through which a person is required to jump–are devised by professionals who, though well-intentioned in their efforts, often give little consideration to the hopes, dreams and desires of the person being served.

The standard training model confronts the trainee with ordered goals and task-analyzed steps–maps of the territory that she has to master. Life is not like that. There is no curriculum for "Get a Life 101." There is no assessment that can measure the skills needed to make a friend, lend a hand or take a stand. We do not learn those things by constructing a match with the preexisting template. Instead, we approach mastery of any given task by meeting the challenges raised by the opportunity to engage with that task. Each time we meet the challenge, we enhance our ability to rise to a new occasion.

Learning Through Participation

Imagine going on a hike to a barely accessible canyon through hot, dry, dangerous country. Along the way, you encounter rivers that you do not know how or where to cross and strange, unfamiliar animals that might be dangerous. You could prepare for such a trip by attending a course on desert travel taught by a renowned expert at a leading university. You could study desert flora and fauna, survival techniques, geology and meteorology. You could probably earn a master's degree in survival technology for arid lands.

Or you could just hire a guide, someone who knows the territory and is willing to go with you. The guide could keep you out of trouble, point you in the right direction and give you wise tips along the way. With such a guide, you could take the trip next week; you would not have to postpone the trip until after you got your degree in "desertology." There would be no prerequisite to identify three poisonous animals and their habitats, no qualifying requirement that you demonstrate the ability to extract water from a cactus in order to prove that you are ready for the trip. Would you learn a lot about desert flora and fauna, survival techniques, geology and meteorology along the way? Of course! You would soak up everything your guide knows about this strange world. You would learn it in the soles of your feet and the base of your brain.

Why should the process be any different for people who are trying to get a life, whose exotic journey is the sometimes long and difficult road to inclusion?

Teaching Techniques

One technique of classical Learning Theory, which has been applied to people with disabilities, bears the forbidding name "shaping behavior through successive approximations." Often known as *successive approximation*, this technique acknowledges the fact that we develop little pieces of abilities in a random and seemingly disorganized fashion. Specifically, each time we attempt a task, we get a little closer to successful completion of it. This technique can be applied very effectively to participatory learning.

Unfortunately, the principle of successive approximation has been systematized into the *backward chaining* method of teaching. In backward chaining, we structure a complex task into small steps. Then, we train a person on one step at a time, from the last to the first, chaining behaviors together in a backward fashion until the trainee can complete the whole task. Each trial of the task is intended to be a little closer to the ideal. Each attempt approximates the completed task, and a succession of these approximations ultimately accomplishes the entire task. This is a neat theory, and almost everyone who has been involved in skill acquisition for people with intellectual disabilities in the last thirty years has engaged in this kind of training.

However, the backward chaining model is intrinsically flawed. For one thing, people often plateau on one of the steps. For example, a trainee cannot put on her shoes because she is unable to pull the tongue of the shoe up. So, she must continue to practice pulling the tongue. She does not get credit for the other parts of the task she already knows how to do because the goal is to learn a logical sequence of skills. She must learn it the way the teacher says it should be learned. If access to our desert hike were controlled through a backward chaining model, we would not get to go if we could not pass Step 6: "Memorize twenty-four desert plants and their traditional medicinal uses."

In recent years, the *total task method* has gained professional preference over successive approximation and backward chaining. This

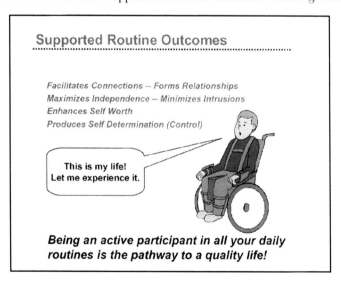

Supported Routine Outcomes

Facilitates Connections -- Forms Relationships
Maximizes Independence -- Minimizes Intrusions
Enhances Self Worth
Produces Self Determination (Control)

This is my life! Let me experience it.

Being an active participant in all your daily routines is the pathway to a quality life!

approach, based on studies of incidental learning from the mid 1970s, comes closer to the way we more commonly learn new things–as whole tasks. Instead of teaching skills piecemeal, the instructor assists the learner in steps during the entire task, giving only as much help and guidance as is required, encouraging the maximum amount of independence throughout the whole undertaking. The task is still structured as a series of distinct sub-tasks, but all the parts are rehearsed each time the person does the task.

Analysis into parts serves to facilitate the trainer's assessment of progress made, not to facilitate the learning process itself. Each time the trainee engages in the task, the trainer keeps track of how much assistance or support the learner needed on each element of the activity. A scoring system is used to measure the degree of participation–for example, how much the learner was able to do on his own and how much assistance was needed. The total task method is still a fairly formal teacher/student kind of arrangement, but it more closely resembles the "opportunities for learning" ideal than the backward chaining approach.

Offering Support

The next conceptual leap in the evolution of our ability to enhance the learning process is to forgo the notion of training tasks entirely. (With this leap, we are still not addressing the deeper issues of life enhancement.) Instead, we are guided by the maxim, "Take what you can get closest to what you want" (attributed to educator and advocate Lee Graber). This maxim acknowledges that we need to accept successive approximations of the skills people want to learn. The hope is that each time a person participates in an activity, she will get a little closer to doing it "right."

MAXIM: *Take what you can get closest to what you want.*
– *Lee Graber*

We initiate this new approach to assisting people to learn new skills by putting ourselves in the role of guide, mentor, ally and coach.

For example, we may be confronted with the task of offering support to a person who does not know how to prepare a meal. It is not our job to teach that person how to cook supper in the sense of offering a series of lessons. Nor are *we* to cook the supper with that person's help. Instead, we must accept the challenge by offering only as much guidance and support as is necessary for him to participate fully in cooking his own supper. We must shift our role from that of teacher to that of caring supporter.

MAXIM: *To do for nurtures dependency – dependency nurtures to do for.* ™

There is a paradigm shift here–an important change in the way we look at the processes and protocols of learning. Though we are assisting and supporting the person with whom we are working, it is important for us to constantly keep in mind that it is *his* supper, *his* kitchen, *his* chore and *his* life, regardless of how much support he may require. Our job, our obligation, is to offer whatever help and guidance may be necessary at the moment, and no more. We are neither "doing to" nor "doing for;" we are "doing with."

For example, if Mary has very limited use of her arms, has severe visual impairment and uses a wheelchair for mobility, she is likely to require a fair amount of support when she decides to cook some macaroni and cheese. She may need adapted cooking utensils, a lowered stovetop or the supports offered through graduated guidance. Regardless of the supports she may require, we are going to celebrate Mary's participation, whatever that may be, in the process of cooking her macaroni and cheese dinner. We are going to take what we can get closest to what we want.

Thinking Out Loud

In some cases, when a person's participation is severely limited by cognitive, physical or behavioral challenges, we can accomplish this goal through the use of a simple technique called thinking out loud.

When we use this technique, we talk naturally and continually with the person about what we are doing together, engaging the person in the task if on no other level than conversation about the task. We share with them our thoughts, ideas, solutions to problems, feelings of frustration, and so on. When we are thinking out loud, we are not only offering the person information about elements of the task at hand, but are also bonding with that person in a relationship of equality and reciprocity. The distinction of roles falls away as we *do the task together*.

MAXIM: *Never assist a person in moving without his or her permission.*

I may say, "Mary, you said you wanted to cook some macaroni and cheese tonight. Would you like for me to give you a hand?"

Mary may never have spoken any words, but with a struggle, she lifts her head and gives me a bit of a smile. I interpret that as a yes. I accept her way of acknowledging because that is all she can provide right now.

I then ask, "Mary, are you ready to go into the kitchen and get your supplies together?" If Mary is unable to independently turn the wheels

Think Out Loud

Make a conscious effort to talk with the person who does not speak. Focus on current activities, or share your thoughts.

Bob, it really looks like a beautiful day today.

By thinking aloud, we:
- facilitate and promote the person's verbal skills
- set a foundation for bonding
- behave courteously
- sharpen our awareness that we are not interacting with an inanimate object.

of her wheelchair, I ask her if I may assist her. If she can push some, I give only the assistance she requires. If she can push herself slowly, I tell her I will meet her in the kitchen, and I allow her time to get there. I welcome Mary's participation in whatever form it takes. I affirm her effort. I take what I can get closest to what we both want: increased participation and an enhanced ability to affect her environment.

In the kitchen, I might say, "Mary, let's get the macaroni and cheese box down." Perhaps she cannot independently reach the cupboard because her home is not yet adapted to meet her needs. I may need to do most of the reaching. Even if we contribute ninety-five percent of the total activity to Mary's five percent (though Mary's effort may actually be greater), it is critical that we perceive our role as that of assistant or support to Mary.

I may continue, "Will you hold that for a minute, and I'll get the pan we need?" She can hold the box in her lap. "Is this the right size pan, or do you think we need a larger one? I think this one will do. Let's see that box. How many cups will this make?" Everything I do, I think out loud. I am sharing the task with Mary, not doing it for her. I am not running a ten-step kitchen skills training program. I must constantly remind myself that this is Mary's task; I am just a support and a guide.

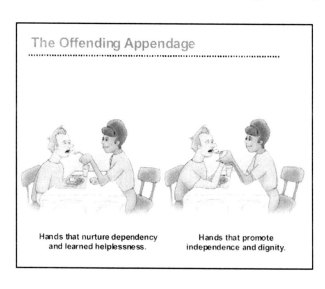

The Offending Appendage

Hands that nurture dependency and learned helplessness.

Hands that promote independence and dignity.

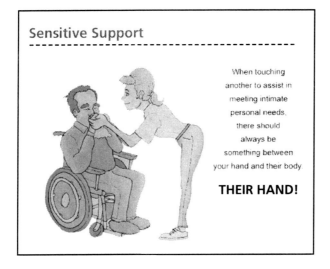

> **Sensitive Support**
>
> When touching another to assist in meeting intimate personal needs, there should always be something between your hand and their body.
>
> **THEIR HAND!**

I may need to assist Mary so intensively that it appears I am the one completing most of the task, but at no time will I allow myself the indulgence of thinking, "I know she can't do this, so I'll do it for her." I always offer her the opportunity to do and to learn. I never "do for." I am not going to go into the kitchen by myself, lay out all the materials for macaroni and cheese, put the water in the measuring cup, open the box, then call Mary in to pour the box's contents and the water into the pan.

MAXIM: *All activities (routines) have a beginning and an end. Do not deny the person his right to participate from the beginning to the end.*

If I did that, Mary would not be cooking her supper; she would be working on a step in a training program. I would deprive her of the opportunity to participate in her own life. And, I would forfeit an opportunity to bond with Mary in an ever-growing relationship.

It does not matter whether the cause of Mary's need for support is an intellectual disability, cerebral palsy, Alzheimer's disease, severe schizophrenia or social deprivation. All of those conditions, and

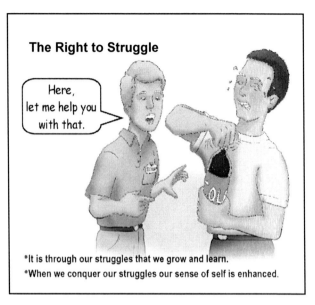

others, serve as barriers to a person's learning how to fix macaroni and cheese independently. But, none is an obstacle to participating in all activities of life right now—even fixing supper. All that is needed is the right kind of support. We call this notion that you learn by participating the *principle of immersion*. It states that a person does not have to be prepared for a task through simulated training activities prior to engaging in it. Rather, the person must learn the necessary skills through immersion in the task at hand.

For instance, you do not have to learn to speak French in order to go to France. On the contrary, when you are in France, surrounded by residents who speak French, seemingly handicapped because you only know the words for "bathroom," "church" and "hello," your knowledge of the language will explode in wonderful varieties of application. In the French milieu, the people who take the time to listen to your halting attempts at communicating in French are caring supporters. This immersion is a cornerstone of the new paradigm of Universal Enhancement.

In addition to thinking out loud, an important skill for supporting a person's maximum level of participation is the use of an effective *prompting sequence.* Also known as graduated guidance, the prompting sequence assures that we only provide as much assistance as a person needs in order to maximize his or her participation.

TOOLBOX
The Prompting Sequence: Ask, Show, Assist

The technical terms for the prompting sequence are *verbal prompt*, *gestural prompt* and *physical prompt*. Simply stated, they are:
- Ask
- Show
- Assist

This sequence is easy to use and should become a natural part of our relationship when assisting and supporting people.

First, **Ask** the person to do the task at hand: "John, would you please put your shoes away?" You then give John a minute to respond to your cue.

If he does not respond, you **Show** him how to do it. Point at his shoes and the closet. Or, model the task by putting a different pair of shoes away.

If John still does not respond, you **Assist** him. Use gentle hand-over-hand guidance to help him do the task. It is crucial to understand that offering physical guidance does not mean making a person do something he does not want to do. (A response of non-cooperation requires providing "motivation," a different form of assistance.)

MAXIM: *If you make it a struggle, you will lose. We all lose.*

Physical assistance is a way of offering support by actually showing the person how to move his limbs to complete the task.

It is very important that acknowledgment and celebration of success (reinforcement) follow each time the person does the task, regardless of how much assistance was needed. We all try harder and achieve more in an atmosphere of recognition and praise. Even if you have to mold John's hand to the shoe and move his arm to the closet, he still puts away his shoes, thereby participating in his own life. Next, you need to tell him so: "Thanks, John, for putting away your shoes. You did great!"

Doing It With

"Taking what we can get" can be coupled here with another maxim. The two of them comprise all of the teaching techniques we need in most situations. The second maxim is "Never do anything by yourself–do it *with*." (Exceptions are going to the bathroom and smoking a cigarette.)

MAXIM: *Never do anything by yourself other than go to the bathroom or smoke a cigarette.* ™

Most staff, as well as most Normative moms, dads and friends, are capable of making macaroni and cheese from a box independently. But that is not their job. They are not direct care staff who are charged with caring for people with disabilities who lack the ability to take care of themselves. They are people whose role is that of support and guide. The only chores that can be owned by our paid staff are the ones we tack on as administrative duties, tasks like data collection and record keeping. *All household tasks belong to and are the responsibility of those who live in the household.* The staff should never deny a person who lives in his own home an opportunity (his right) to experience life and garner the skills that serve to enhance the quality of his life by doing these tasks for him.

I once observed a group home staff person vacuuming the living room while three of the men who lived in the home sat passively in a line on the sofa. When the staff person approached the sofa with the vacuum cleaner, the three men simultaneously lifted their feet while she cleaned under them. She was denying them the opportunity to participate in keeping their own house clean.

This denial of opportunity cannot be compensated by assigning each of the men to a "vacuuming program" to be conducted at eight p.m. each Tuesday and Thursday. Such a program fails to address the fact that part of learning a task is learning the time and place of its occurrence, the natural rhythm of the event. Most of us vacuum the rugs when they are dirty or when we get an opportunity to catch up on our cleaning (as the staff person was doing). How many of us vacuum the rugs at precisely eight p.m. each Tuesday and Thursday?

The question posed is not can, will, or should the person participate in life's activities, but *how*. What assistance and support is necessary to allow this person the opportunity for full participation?

MAXIM: *Every reason that you give why you don't, is the justification for doing it.* ™

It should be evident by now that the Medical/Custodial Model of "care for" is quickly being relegated to the historical archives. Behind us, too, is the model focused on assessing where on a developmental chart the person's cooking skills fall. And, we are rapidly progressing beyond the Habilitation Model, which focuses on the assessment of

---

He Can't Because

- *Every reason that you give why one shouldn't is the justification for doing it!*
- *He can't do it because:*
  - he is too contractured
  - he lacks a pincer grasp
  - she is unsteady in her gait
  - she engages in pica behavior
  - she is on a salt restricted diet
  - he becomes agitated when requested to participate
  - he tires easily

strengths and needs as a mechanism for determining whether a person is ready to master those skills that would allow them to move to a less restrictive environment.

When we use the principle of taking what you can get closest to what you want, everyone is ever-ready for everything. Everyone, regardless of ability, can choose his or her place of residence and have his or her own home. Everyone can perform real work and earn real compensation without regard to "work readiness skills."

TALE
It's Alfred's Lunch

After having conducted Universal Enhancement training at a large "developmental center," I walked into the dining room where eighty-five people were having their lunch. At the edge of a crowd of people waiting their turn to go through the serving line, I saw Alfred, sitting in his wheelchair, head down, not moving, silent.

Alfred has cerebral palsy and requires pervasive supports, including a special chair with postural inserts. He has difficulty lifting his head to focus on objects in his environment. He does not speak.

While I was watching, Christy, one of the staff people who had not attended the training, walked up behind Alfred's wheelchair and began to move him across the room as if she were pushing a wheelbarrow with a load of firewood. She pushed Alfred up to the table without saying anything, and "parked" him there by locking both wheels of his chair.

Christy then headed toward the kitchen to get Alfred his lunch. So I asked, "Why are you getting Alfred his lunch? He can do it himself."

Her response, within Alfred's hearing, was, "Alfred can't get his own lunch; he's too retarded."

I was really taken aback by this, so I took Christy aside and said, "I understand you were not able to attend this morning's training, but I see here an opportunity to put some of the principles I talked about into practice. Would you mind working with me on a couple of things?"

She rolled her eyes and gestured that she felt she didn't have a choice but would let me proceed. She probably wondered if she was going to get credit for this impromptu training.

"First of all," I told Christy, in a low enough tone of voice that none of her coworkers could hear, "we should never talk about people in front of them. We don't know what Alfred understands, but we surely want to be sensitive to his feelings and treat him the way we would want to be treated.

"And secondly, Alfred is more than capable of getting his own lunch. We just have to accept the fact that he's going to need some assistance and support. Why don't we go into the kitchen with Alfred and help him get his lunch?"

So, Christy again went up behind Alfred, grabbed his wheelchair and started to head for the kitchen.

I said, "Wait a minute. Before you do that, why don't we tell Alfred where we're going and what we're doing, and get his permission to do it."

Christy looked at me with a gaze of puzzlement and contempt, turned to Alfred and said in a voice devoid of emotion, "Alfred, this man says I have to tell you what I'm doing. I'm going to take you into the kitchen."

I took what I could get closest to what I want–Christy's willingness to talk to Alfred was a start.

Now, I don't know whether Alfred understands spoken communication or not, but as we were walking toward the kitchen, I said, "Alfred, doesn't that smell good? I'm not sure what it is. What does that smell like to you? Pork chops and some kind of stuffing? I like that. Maybe we're going to have mashed potatoes, too. Are you hungry? I'm really hungry." I continued talking to Alfred as we entered a large, commercial kitchen.

I then turned to Christy and said, "Would you like to help Alfred get his lunch?" She looked at me in confusion, having learned already that it was not acceptable to say Alfred is too retarded. She still didn't know what to do. So I asked her if I could help. She nodded her head.

I walked up next to Alfred and asked, "Alfred, can I help you pick out some lunch today?" Then I helped him get a tray and go to the first station in the serving line.

As I pulled the bowl of mashed potatoes down from the shelf, I asked Alfred, "Would you like some mashed potatoes? Let me help you get them." So I put the serving spoon in his hand, and though his range of motion was pretty limited, I helped him put potatoes on his plate.

Then we came to the stuffing, and I said, "This stuff smells pretty good. You want some of this dressing? It smells like it has sage in it." (I had to hold it so he could smell it.) Then, I helped him put some of it on his plate.

I turned again to Christy and asked her if she would like to continue to help Alfred with his lunch, and there was an amazed look on her face. I could see that she understood. She had never thought of Alfred as a real person before. She had seen him as a work unit. "Feeding Alfred" had been one of the tasks she had to accomplish every day. When the paradigm shift hit her–that Alfred could do anything with the right kind of support and assistance, and that she was that support and assistance–a whole new world of engagement opened up for her and for Alfred.

Christy may not have gotten the whole picture that day. She may not have understood all the things that Alfred could have been learning through the simple act of choosing his lunch–matching smells with words; and improving auditory attention, visual tracking and palmar grasp.

I do hope she realized, though, that Alfred learned more through participating in getting his lunch than he would have had she left him "parked" in the cafeteria while she got food for him. I think she also began to understand that by taking what she could get closest to what she wanted she was encouraging Alfred to be as independent as he could possibly be, while at the same time opening up a world of experience and relationship for both of them.

The question is not whether a person is ready to have a life; the question is "How much support will this person need?" The only way we can answer that question is by interacting and engaging with people who have been cast aside, assuring opportunities and supporting their efforts to participate in all the activities of their lives, offering only as much assistance as they require, and no more.

MAXIM: *You do not have to prove yourself to have a reasonable life.*

We say, "Take what you can get closest to what you want," but we really mean, "Offer the amount of support that allows the people we work with to get as close as they can to what they want." In this model, the people receiving the support are always in charge. They are constantly on a quest to acquire the skills and competencies they want to develop, as part of realizing their hopes, dreams and desires.

3

Obstacles to Opportunities

7

Supported Routines

Section 2, *Challenging the Gatekeepers*, reviewed the premise that the Habilitation Model of service provision pursues habilitation as a goal with movement to a less restrictive environment as the *earned* result. The principles of Universal Enhancement put a new twist on that equation.

The habilitation process provides opportunities for learning and the means by which a person may grow, develop and become more independent despite his or her Outsider status. But, habilitation is a result, not a goal. Habilitation results from being an active participant in life. Being afforded an opportunity to participate in all of one's daily routines with necessary supports assures a high level of engagement. And, a level of engagement requires interaction with the materials of life, what is called *media*.

MAXIM: *Habilitation is not a goal; it is a result.* ™

This sounds like a rather complex process, but it is really just a compact formulation of the way we all acquire new abilities. We learn new skills by being engaged with the objects we encounter in our life activities. That is what media is–*stuff*–things, objects and people–all of the thousands of physical entities that surround and enrich our lives.

Think back to your childhood. How did you learn to vacuum? Did someone put you on a rug vacuuming program? Not likely. You prob-

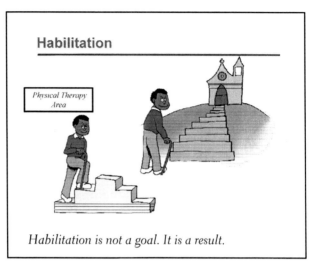

Habilitation is not a goal. It is a result.

ably first interacted with a vacuum cleaner (media) by watching Mom or Dad use it. Maybe you touched it while it was standing in the middle of the living room. If you saw someone plug it in or turn it on, you may have tried that. If there had been no vacuum cleaners in your environment, you would have had no way of learning how to operate one.

The acquisition of language is another good example of how we learn new skills through supported routines. Children are seldom

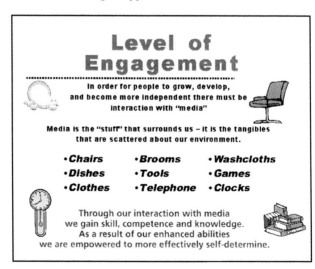

taught to talk through formal instruction. Instead, they are surrounded by language–spoken, written, gestured and sung. They are engaged with it and immersed in it all day long. Children absorb language by interacting with it.

In environments with institutional characteristics, the media is scarce, restricted or contrived. Most of the *stuff* of everyday life is not available for engagement by the persons who live there. It is, instead, owned by, or under the control of, various staff who provide assorted services. The vacuum cleaners are locked up for the sole use of the staff, who vacuum after everyone who lives there is in bed or has left the home for his or her day program.

The food preparation items are in the kitchen that is operated by the staff. The washers and dryers sit behind locked doors, operated by staff. Maintenance personnel bring their tools to the job when they change the light bulbs and unstop the toilets.

Lest this description seem limited to the environment of the large, state-operated facility, let us look at a few limitations that even occur in community-based residences. The dining room table has no napkin holder because Terry eats any paper products she can get her hands on. The TV set is locked up because Dwayne is fascinated with electronics

---

UE Markers

These strongly indicate that the UE standard is being met. It's the type of place I would like to live!
- Magazines or eye-catching books in magazine rack next to the toilet
- Cookie or candy jar with tempting items—always accessible
- Adaptive devices in abundance—long-handled feather dusters, wash mitts, jelly bean switches, pump coffee pots, comprehensive home chore list (faithfully followed)
- Women wearing makeup daily—perhaps a purple stripe in their hair
- Possession and use of sunglasses, raincoats and umbrellas
- Alarm clocks on all night stands—routinely used
- All individuals possess and carry billfolds—they "don't leave home without them."
- Residents of the home welcome guests and offer them a beverage.

and takes things apart. The front door is locked so that Melissa will not suddenly run out into the street. In many small, congregate residential or sheltered employment settings, you will see this repeated.

MAXIM: *The person with the most challenging behavior determines the least restrictive environment.*

In lieu of the usual serendipitous access to common media, sometimes special training areas are established. These program rooms, or activities of daily living rooms, are simulation areas in which "clients" can interact with media while they do their scheduled training programs. The vacuum cleaner may be removed from the storage closet if a person has a vacuuming goal on his IHP.

Someone may be presented with items of differing texture in the sensory integration rooms. People get together to practice social interaction skills in the social skills training area. The place looks like a normal living room but is actually located in a building different from the one in which these participants live.

Training is contrived in such situations, and learning does not come about in the way most of us have naturally experienced it—through our daily interaction with a lot of *stuff*.

By their very nature, typical institutional settings provide minimal opportunities to interact with media. There is not much stuff available, and items that are present are usually only accessible at appointed times, with designated supervision.

Supported Routines

When people are not active participants in their daily routines, some very unpleasant things occur. Where there is little to do and not much *stuff* with which to do it, people will more often than not use their creativity to devise nonproductive and/or destructive activities. A human being must always exhibit some kind of behavior; he or she must be doing something regardless of how sparse the environment.

We should not be surprised, therefore, when a man who lives in a barren, institutional environment steals a handful of rice from the plate of a man seated nearby at the Chinese restaurant. Who can blame the woman with no control over most facets of her life for kicking us in the shins? Where there are minimal opportunities, decreased choices and lack of control in one's environment, alternative behaviors are more likely to develop.

Where there are limited opportunities to be an active participant in one's daily routines, it is likely there will be an increase in the following behaviors.

1. *Stereotypical behavior.* This is the sort of purposeless, repetitive motion that is so striking to the first-time visitor to any institutional setting. People rock, moan or wave their hands in front of their eyes like some endless, predictable, idiosyncratic dance.
2. *Self-injurious behavior.* People slap themselves, bite their hands and arms, or hit their heads against the wall or floor repeatedly.
3. *Aggression.* People assault their peers and staff by hitting, kicking, biting, spitting or throwing objects.
4. *Property damage.* People engage in destructive behavior ranging from picking little pieces out of a chair or shredding their clothes, to breaking windows and furniture, or tearing doors off their hinges.

> **TOOLBOX**
> **Supported Routine Outcomes**
>
> Facilitates connections – Forms relationships
> Maximizes independence – Minimizes intrusions
> Enhances self-worth – Produces self-determination (control)

All of these behaviors are likely to show up in any setting that denies people the opportunity for active involvement and participation with their environment. These behaviors are almost always present in settings designed to serve Outsiders; this includes state hospitals, nursing homes and juvenile detention centers (with some stylistic differences, depending on the population).

It is reasonable, therefore, to conclude that behaviors such as those listed above are not characteristic of any particular group of Outsiders. Though it is embarrassing to admit it, I used to believe that they were characteristics of a particular group of Outsiders, that such behaviors were symptoms of a person's diagnosis.

MAXIM: *We must provide an environment that is healthy enough for a life to happen. –Dan Berkwicz*

Seldom, however, is there genetic damage, brain dysfunction or other diagnostic entities that cause people to act this way. You may notice striking similarities when you visit a large residential facility for people with mental illness, for elders or for children who have no parents. To varying degrees, you can observe the four alternative behaviors in all of these settings.

In light of such similar behavior, we need to re-examine our stereotypes and come to an almost inescapable new realization. These behaviors occur in places where there is limited opportunity to be actively involved in one's life, regardless of the attributes of the people who live there.

TALE
My TV

I visited a home in which three young men were living. Randy, one of the men, indicated by gestures and vocalizations that he wanted me to see something in his bedroom. I entered Randy's room, and he pointed with pride at a brand new thirteen-inch television set on a table. He kept saying, "My TV. My TV," all the while smiling broadly. I found out later that Randy had purchased the TV with money he had saved from his sheltered workshop income over a period of six months. That TV was his most prized possession.

A couple of months later, I returned to Randy's home. I remembered the new TV, and I asked him about it. He got a sad expression on his face and shook his head in a gesture of negation. One of the staff told me that Randy had gotten angry one evening and smashed his TV set against the bedroom wall.

Why, I wondered, would someone destroy his own property, something he had worked and saved for? The answer, I believe, has to do with the issue of control. There was always one thing he could do to assert himself as somebody. He could smash his own prized TV set out of sheer frustration and rage at a life that allowed little in the way of options and no constructive way to influence his destiny.

This condition of having limited opportunities for meaningful interactions with people and objects in one's life is sometimes referred to as anomie. Literally, anomie means "no law or no name." It comes from the same root as the word anonymous. People who suffer from anomie have no investment in their lives or the lives of the people around them. They do not have the relationships that constitute the warp and woof of community life. They act out the conclusion, "If my life has no meaning or value, I will behave in a way to cause your life to have no meaning or value either."

MAXIM: *If my life has no meaning or value, I will behave in a way to cause your life to have no meaning or value either.*

We have seen examples of anomie in recent historical events. People who live in a bleak, inner city moonscape of empty buildings and empty lives, lacking the opportunity to control their destinies, may act out their anomie by vandalizing, burning and looting. As a society, we are used to tracing the causes of such behavior to poverty, lack of education or violence in the streets. Could it be that the real root of such violent self-destructiveness is an almost total lack of the kinds of options many people take for granted? Adolescents who live in areas of urban blight do not think about what they will be when they grow up; they wonder *if* they will grow up.

MAXIM: *You cannot fix a broken life with a behavior management plan.* ™

Likewise, people who live in bleak institutional environments, whose lives are regimented, directed, programmed and devoid of meaningful options, have little reason to care about the long-range planning strategies necessary for putting together a meaningful life. This is why many of the behavior management plans generated by psychologists do not work. They do not speak to the need for a person to have an impact on his or her own life, to make choices and be somebody.

MAXIM: *If we were all good social workers, we wouldn't need psychologists.* ™

Indeed, among the disciplines that are generally present in services for Outsiders, it is social work which most commonly addresses the needs for autonomy and relationships. If anomie is the cause of challenging behavior, a good social work approach may be the best solution. People who are active participants in their lives are more likely to form meaningful relationships and gain things of value–hobbies, collections, spirituality and employment. Through these experiences, a person is building the foundation to realize his or her preferred future and proclaim, "I am somebody."

Quality of Life Profile

The Quality of Life Profile is a device for assessing and evaluating lifestyles. By plotting on a graph the activities you spend your time on, and considering both the relative value and the importance of personal relationships in those activities, you can gain insight into the style of your life. Are you a solitary person, preferring to do things alone? Or, are you a gregarious, social person to whom relationships with others are an important part of what is valuable in an activity? Do you have lots of activities in your life that are highly valued, or relatively few activities of limited importance? Are you pleased with your lifestyle? Where on the graph would you like to be? How are you going to get there?

Try helping an Outsider create her profile. Does Outsider status tend to put a person in a particular quadrant? Do persons who live with institutional characteristics even have a lifestyle? How does it compare with your lifestyle? What activities, events or opportunities could you support to help an Outsider enhance her quality of life?

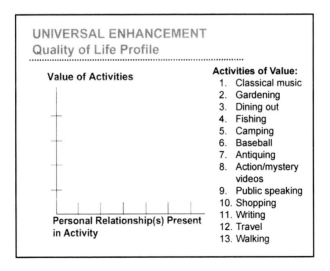

Instructions: Think about the things that you like to do, the activities that bring you personal satisfaction, fulfillment and joy. Now place each activity somewhere on the Quality of Life Profile, following the guidelines below.

The Quality of Life Profile has two scales. On the left (abscissa), progressing from bottom to top, is the scale of the value of your life activities. Those activities you most value would be noted at the top while less valued pastimes would be designated near the bottom. Across the bottom (ordinate) is the scale for the personal relationships involved. An activity you do alone, like reading a magazine or collecting stamps, belongs toward the left-hand side of the line.

Something you do with friends, like playing volleyball or dancing, belongs toward the right-hand side of the line. The scale across the bottom answers the question: How important are *relationships with other people* in this activity?

Use a combination of the two factors to plot each of your chosen activities. If an activity is of low interest and you are indifferent to the presence of other people in the activity, it goes in quadrant C. If, however, you want to record something that is very valuable to you, and the relationships it brings are part of that value, place it in quadrant B.

A VALUE SELF	B ENRICHED (VALUE OTHERS AND ACTIVITIES)
C IMPOVERISHED	D VALUE OTHERS

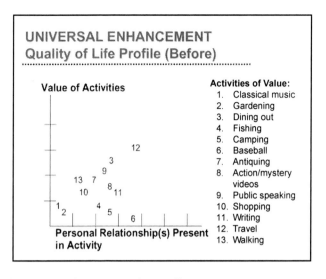

There is no right answer to this profile. It is not a test, but an exercise in self-exploration, designed to give you a picture of the kind of life you lead. The examples illustrate completed profiles depicting one person's quality of life prior to and subsequent to life-enhancing opportunities.

Habilitation = Participation = Universal Enhancement

The usual method of habilitation in an institutional setting is to create places and scheduled times where there is media and the opportunity

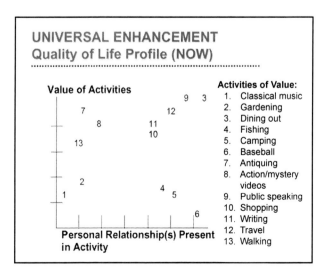

to interact with it. One response is to design activities of daily living (ADL) rooms that have the materials for learning to set a dining table, do laundry or prepare a simple meal. Here the person learns how to perform these tasks in the training room. The idea is that once she can consistently and safely demonstrate all requisite skills in the constructed living area, she can then move from her present residence out to a less restrictive environment where the media for learning are not locked up or broken.

What is often missed here is that movement to a less restrictive environment does not require a physical move from one place to another. A less restrictive environment is not a place. It is an expansion and enhancement of the opportunities and options in a person's life. So, it is time for everyone to move out right now. There are no skill acquisition prerequisites to having the opportunity to have a life—a life that has meaningful activities in the places we normally have them, and a life that has dignity, a life of Universal Enhancement.

Eight Characteristics of Universal Enhancement

Universal Enhancement, like habilitation, is a result of participation in one's own life and the life of the community in which one lives. Universal Enhancement can be applied to any setting and level of abil-

Universal Enhancement Tools

The Tools of Universal Enhancement Are:

* **FREE - not available for purchase.**

* **May be utilized without permission of others**

* **Consistent with existing regulations, policies and procedures**

ity. It is culture-free and location-free. It is a tool to maximize anyone's quality of life. A closer look reveals how this interaction with media can become the foundation for Universal Enhancement. The following eight characteristics have been identified as core or primary characteristics for ensuring a solid foundation for Universal Enhancement. There are many other characteristics, but these are the most important.

Functional

The supported routines must have a function and a purpose. That purpose is to enhance competence and increase a person's ability to adapt to and manage his environment. The person who waves a shoelace in front of his face all day (stereotypical behavior) is certainly engaged with media. But, he learns no adaptive skills from this engagement; the activity is not functional. Skill acquisition, in and of itself, does not necessarily increase a person's ability to adapt to his environment.

TALE
Bertha Reaches Out

Bertha had a stroke that limited her range of motion and her ability to walk independently. A physical therapist prescribed daily range of motion exercises, and staff helped Bertha obtain a walker to help her ambulate in her home. The interdisciplinary team had set vacuuming rugs as a training goal for Bertha for the coming year, but because of Bertha's physical limitations, they decided to postpone this goal until she had attained better motor abilities.

A staff person who provided support to Bertha for a number of years suggested that instead of deferring the training in vacuuming, the team should let it serve as the physical therapy. "When Bertha reaches out with the vacuum cleaner to clean under the couch, she's doing the same thing as those exercises the physical therapist gave her. Why can't she get her exercise by doing the vacuuming?" she asked.

> **Functional Activities**
>
> **What new skills or competencies is the person acquiring?**
>
> **Functional Outcomes**
> - **Range of Motion**
> - **Palmar grasp**
> - **Prepositions**
> - **Following a three-part instruction**
> - **Ambulation**

This alert staff person knew that the best way to develop functional skills is to participate in meaningful activities that require those skills.

But there's more to the story. The staff person also realized that the real reason Bertha needed to increase her range of motion was so she could use her walker more efficiently. And the real reason she wanted to learn to use her walker more efficiently was so she could go shopping with her sister.

Meaningful

It used to be a joke about basic military training that the drill sergeant would have new recruits go out to a field and dig holes, then fill them in again. Was the individual engaged with various media? Of course. The recruit was engaged with the shovel, the dirt and the sergeant. Was it functional; did it teach new skills? Certainly. The recruit could learn how to angle the shovel to get the best dirt load and how far to throw that load so it would not fall back into the hole. He could build his upper body strength and his endurance. He might even learn what happens if he does not follow the sergeant's orders! The task is certainly *functional*. But the recruit is probably wondering how *meaningful* it is.

Outsiders, (people like recruits) are not seen as peers or equals to those who set task expectations. They are often required to engage in activities that have little meaning. Consider the fraternity pledge's chore of scrubbing the kitchen floor with a toothbrush or the tenderfoot Boy Scout's errand to find a "smoke bender."

The test of whether or not the training task is meaningful is to ask the question, "If the person who is engaged in the task was not doing this task, would someone else have to do it?" In other words, is this a real task, or is it just made up for training purposes?

MAXIM: *If the person who is engaged in the task was not doing it, would someone else have to do it?*

Some disability training equivalents of the soldier's hole digging are "beads on a string," "rings on a stick" and "pegs in a pegboard." In the latter task, the person is given a flat board with rows of holes in it and a box of pegs that fit into the holes. They are then required to put the pegs into the holes.

Now, this task does indeed have many potential functional outcomes. The "pegger" can improve eye-hand coordination, pincer

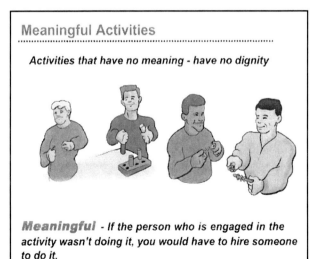

Meaningful Activities

Activities that have no meaning - have no dignity

Meaningful - *If the person who is engaged in the activity wasn't doing it, you would have to hire someone to do it.*

grasp, sequencing, color recognition, attention to task, work endurance, following instructions, and so on. But, is it a real task? If the person being trained were not doing it, would a pegboard technician have to come in and make sure all the pegboards are filled? Of course not. Pegboard filling does not meet the criterion for meaningfulness. The proof of that is that when the person finishes the task, the pegs are removed from the pegboard, put back in the box, and the "pegger" gets to do the task all over again.

To add to the tragedy, their work is usually destroyed in front of them. How would you feel if someone came and destroyed your work when you were finished? You would probably think, "This is stupid." You would probably resist doing it and end up with an "increase on-task behavior" goal on your next IHP.

Giving people meaningless undertakings is demeaning and disrespectful, and it should come as no surprise that people who are subjected to these activities rebel against them in the best way they know how. Tasks that have no meaning have no dignity. Rebellious behavior may be a person's means of communicating the plea, "Treat me with dignity."

Instead of making up meaningless training activities, we must use all of the real, everyday tasks that are readily at hand. Eye-hand coordination can be learned by setting the table. Pincer grasp can be improved by holding a toothbrush. Raking the leaves in the front yard can increase work endurance.

MAXIM: *Tasks that have no meaning have no dignity.*

When skills are taught through participation in real tasks, we do not have to worry about "generalization," the concern about whether the person can apply the newly learned skill to novel situations (in various environments). This concern is only valid if the skill is being learned in an environment different from that in which it is to be applied (learning to dress in a training room, for instance). Meaningful skills are being applied at the time they are being learned.

TALE
My Brother Daryl

My brother, Daryl, has mental retardation. He has been in school for twelve years and has never been served in any setting other than an elementary school. He has had years of "individualized instruction" and can do lots of things he couldn't do before!

He can put one hundred pegs in a board in less than ten minutes while in his seat with ninety-five percent accuracy.

But he can't put quarters in vending machines.

Upon command, he can touch nose, shoulder, leg, foot, hair and ear. He is still working on wrist, ankle and hips.

But he can't blow his nose when needed.

He can do a twelve-piece Big Bird puzzle with one hundred percent accuracy, and color an Easter Bunny and stay in the lines.

But he prefers music and was never taught how to use a radio or tape player.

He can fold primary paper in halves and, even, quarters.

But he can't fold his clothes.

He can sort blocks by colors—up to ten different colors.

But he can't sort clothes, whites from colors, for washing.

He can roll Play-Doh and make wonderful clay snakes.

But he can't roll bread dough and cut out biscuits.

He can string beads in alternating colors and match it to a pattern on a DLM card.

But he can't lace his shoes.

He can sing his ABCs and tell me names of all the letters of the alphabet when presented on a card in upper case with eighty percent accuracy.

But he can't tell the difference between the men's room and the ladies' when we go to a restaurant.

When he is told it's cloudy/rainy, he can take a black felt cloud and put it on the day of the week on an enlarged calendar without assistance.

But he still goes out in the rain without a raincoat or hat.

He can identify with one hundred percent accuracy one hundred different Peabody Picture Cards by pointing.

But he can't order a hamburger by pointing to a picture or gesturing.

He can walk a balance beam frontward, sideways and backward.

But he can't walk up the steps of the bleachers unassisted in the gym or go to a basketball game.

He can count to one hundred by rote memory.

But he doesn't know how many dollars to pay the waitress for a $2.59 McDonald's special.

He can put a cube "in" the box, "under" the box, "beside" the box and "behind" the box.

But he can't find the trash bin in the cafeteria and empty his trash.

He can sit in a circle with appropriate behavior, sing songs and play Duck Duck Goose.

But nobody else his age in our neighborhood seems to want to do that.

I guess he's just not ready yet.

Reprinted from The Cutting Edge, October 1987. Author unknown.

Normalized Rhythm

One of the things learned from the routines of our day is when to begin and end our various tasks. We brush our teeth in the morning or after meals, and flush the toilet after using it. We cook our food just before mealtime. We get dressed when we get up and undressed when we go to bed. Our lives have a rhythm, a context, a logical sequence. One activity or event triggers initiation of the next.

When we teach people tasks at training time, a time chosen because of scheduling needs rather than a response to the rhythms of life, we do not allow them to learn the flow and pace of daily events. Such an approach inhibits the recognition of the interconnectedness of activities and tasks, that one event leads to something else happening. We go to bed, for instance, because we are sleepy, our work is done, we have to get up early for work in the morning or because the TV news is over.

We do not turn in because it is eight-thirty p.m., bedtime on the master schedule. The "by the clock" approach is not only demeaning–in that we would not impose a rigid schedule on someone we considered to be our equal–it is also counterproductive. When we do not assist people to learn the rhythm of things, we will always have to schedule and prompt them, keeping them dependent on us.

One aspect of the learned helplessness seen in many people who have lived for years in institutional settings is that they stop self-initiating. They are so accustomed to being scheduled according to the convenience of staffing patterns that they have never learned to schedule

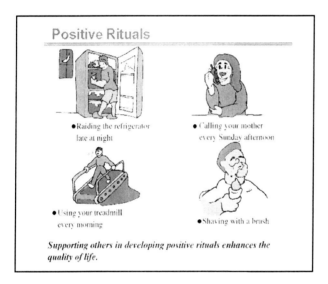

themselves according to the flow of a daily routine. When the rhythms of a person's life are determined by paid staff or concerned caretakers, the tail is wagging the dog.

Age Appropriate
This issue is dealt with in more depth in Chapter 9, but it is important to consider some of the ramifications of using age-appropriate media when we are trying to achieve habilitative outcomes through a level of engagement.

The Tail Should Not Wag the Dog

Dog labeled with:
- Individualization
- Spontaneous activities
- Access to personal fund
- Preferred foods
- Positive rituals
- Intimate relationships

Tail labeled with:
- Staff schedules
- Staff assignments
- Menus
- Fiscal Policies
- Group schedules
- Bulk purchasing
- Licensure regulations

If the media, the *stuff*, used for teaching adults new tasks is the kind that young children commonly use, we will almost certainly limit our expectations of what the adult can do. For example, we have seen artists with intellectual disabilities produce fine, expressive paintings using oil paints on canvas. What would we have seen if we had only allowed them to use crayons and a "Beauty and the Beast" coloring book? We would probably have been focused on whether he or she stayed in the lines and got the color of the sky right. If we are complaisant about Joe, who plays with a stuffed dinosaur at age twenty-seven, will we be likely to take the time to help him learn how to operate a CD player?

Adults generally have a larger set of options than children do. When we surround an adult who has limited competence with the kinds of things an adult usually has access to, he will learn how to use those things. He may develop the skills and competencies he needs for a more satisfying life. We should not settle for a perpetual childish game of pretend, but rather make sure we enrich a person's environment with real things that have real uses.

Participating as Equals

We need a vision of "teaching" that goes beyond the model of the teacher walking around the room giving instructions to students. Our new vision is one of full participation (modeling) as the key to learning. If "students" are doing real tasks with real media at an appropriate time, we should all be more than willing to participate as equals with the persons we are supposedly teaching. Only when we try to get people to do silly, meaningless things do we lose all desire to be involved.

Once again, we are faced with the distinction between teaching and providing opportunities to learn. We provide opportunities by supporting people who are learning how to do new things. We give them just as much support and assistance as they need, but no more. We serve as role models, participating with the person in order to understand how it should be done, rather than standing over them in the role of instructor.

When working in residential settings, support staff should sit down at the table and eat with the people who live there. This allows the staff to model appropriate mealtime behavior, including the wonderful communicative interaction that can take place around the dinner table. Mealtime is an opportunity to share, give, take and review the activities of the day. None of the fine stories would take place if the staff were posted like guards or waiters around the perimeter of the dining room, waiting for the chance to catch someone spilling her milk or stealing a biscuit from her neighbor.

MAXIM: *Don't take people for a walk. Walk with them.*

Ultimately, we wish to see complete inclusion in a vital community, where natural supports (unpaid friends, neighbors and coworkers) prevail and there is no need for paid staff. We can start the process by minimizing the distinction between trainer and trainee, teacher and student, staff and client. The barriers between people will tumble as we participate in all activities of life as equals with people we support.

In the Appropriate Environment

Different events and activities take place in different locations. We get dressed in the bedroom, brush our teeth in the bathroom, cook

Teach the skill in the environment where you want it exercised.

in the kitchen and vacuum where the dirt is. We learned these tasks by seeing others do them and by being given the opportunity to participate in them.

Environments are rich with cues that tell us how and when to act. When we stand at the crosswalk at a busy intersection, for example, we see and hear not only the "walk/don't walk" signs but also the other people. We see them crossing or not crossing, and looking in the direction in which they expect to see traffic. We see the traffic stopping or turning with perhaps a driver slowing for a turn and gesturing us to cross ahead of him.

This multiplicity of events, each one containing some information relevant to whether it is safe for us to cross, cannot be duplicated by the erection of a fake traffic light on an institutional back street. Nor is it duplicated by the selection of the walk symbol from a collection of cardboard training tools presented in the dining room during the pedestrian safety training program.

It is not surprising, then, that people who train others in fake environments wonder whether the person will generalize the skill in a natural environment. When the surroundings in which training occurs are contrived and artificial, a person who has difficulty learning will often be overwhelmed by the cues that are present in any real world situation. The trainers are then left wondering why the person who performed so well during the training program using the shopping trip board game wanders off in a daze during a trip to the mall.

Another reason for learning skills in the environment in which they are to be practiced is that people with intellectual disabilities often have difficulty discriminating subtle distinctions between environments. For instance, if it is deemed acceptable for a man to walk out of the bathroom at this group home with his pants around his knees while attempting to find someone in the living room to help him pull them up, he might think it is appropriate to do the same thing when he walks out of the bathroom at McDonald's or the library.

MAXIM: *Teach the skill in the environment where it is to be exercised.*

The most effective way a person we support can learn that there are definite places for different activities is to participate in them, in the locations where we live, work and play–locations that contain many rich and subtle cues that we respond to regularly.

> **A Level of Engagement Becomes Habilitation When it Meets These Eight Characteristics:**
>
> - Functional
> - Meaningful
> - Normalized rhythm
> - Age appropriate
> - Staff participate as equals
> - Conducted in appropriate environment
> - Individual participates from beginning to end
> - The engagement must be consequated

Engaged from Beginning to End

The necessity of dealing with this issue is a remnant of the old backward chaining training technique. If a person we were working with was on Step 3 of her dusting program—"applies rag to tabletop in circular fashion"—we used to gather all the materials required, spray the cleaning compound on the table, hand the trainee the rag, and say, "Dust the table, Eleanor." When she met the stipulated criterion, she would then be allowed (ready) to move on to the next step—"sprays cleaning compound onto table." It might be a while before she is permitted to "gather materials."

As noted in the previous section, total task learning is preferred. It is complete immersion in the entirety of any activity. It is crucial that the person who is learning a new skill learn the whole skill from beginning to end. Eleanor has the right to participate in the total task. Not only will she possibly need to dust her own table someday and need to know how to do it independently, but also, every task presents opportunities for functional learning that should not be missed (for example, ambulation, pincer grasp, eye-hand coordination, letting go). For instance, if Eleanor has limited use of her hands, taking the cap off the sprayer, pointing it in the right direction, pushing down on the button and letting it go are all occasions for learning. We should not turn our backs on the wealth of learning opportunities contained in what appears to be a simple task.

MAXIM: *Support people at the level they are capable or willing to participate.* ™

A final reason for total task learning is that if a person is not participating in the task, he is probably waiting for someone to do it for him. Unfortunately, though waiting is not a meaningful life activity, many people living in institutional settings spend a good deal of time doing just that—waiting for dinner, a bath or bedtime; waiting for someone else to move their lives to the next activity. People who wait are being deprived. Often, this deprivation is meted out by well-

When your well is full, there is much to give.

meaning staff who still see themselves as caretakers, responsible for providing their "charges" with opportunities to participate in the activities of their own lives.

Consequated

We are all motivated by the appreciation we receive for our efforts from significant others. People need to know that they are doing a good job, their effort is valued, and their willingness to try is recognized even when it ends in failure. This is particularly true of people whose natural curiosity and ambition have been sapped by the enervating anonymity of institutional living. These Outsiders need a special message that they are persons who have value in this world. Therefore, when a person finishes a task, every supported routine must include acknowledgment that the task was completed, praise for a good attempt or a job well done, and the message that the person is appreciated and valued.

Some people, however, experience serious difficulty in their attempts to offer praise. They may have grown up in households where praise was withheld, and scolding and shaming were the rule of the day. They may carry a constant voice within them (one that may sound remarkably like a parent) that says, "It's not perfect. She doesn't deserve praise." People who were not praised as children often have

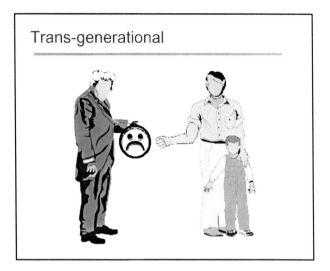

great difficulty praising their own children, and the cycle continues from generation to generation (transgenerational). It is important to realize that we must have "water in our wells" to be able to praise another person for a good attempt or even a job well done. If we feel insecure, unworthy and unrecognized ourselves, it is very difficult to give the needed consequences. If you find yourself in this tragic circumstance, it is imperative that you praise anyway, especially when it is difficult.

MAXIM: *Fake it 'til you make it.*

You can always "fake it 'til you make it"–pretend that you feel good about yourself. Recognizing and celebrating the strivings of another person can generate new feelings of self-esteem in you. When you share with the people you support, you take a giant step along the path of Universal Enhancement.

If we are not hampered by a transgenerational lack of appreciation, we are probably accustomed to offering opportunities to, and praising even the small attempts of, our children. When my daughter was little, I took her outside to teach her how to shoot a basketball

through the hoop. The first time she tried, she just threw the ball in the air without even aiming at the basket. I did not say, "Amy, that's not the way; you're not even facing the right direction!" I said, "Amy, that's wonderful. You threw the basketball!" I praised what was her best effort. We must not worry that the person failed to do the whole task, or did not do it perfectly. We can take what is closest to what we want. We all have to start somewhere.

There is nothing complicated about the praising of successive approximations. We only need to present opportunities and then be willing to support people as their independent participation is enhanced a little bit at a time. We meet the person where she is, joining with her in a collaborative effort. We are not judging her by some arbitrary pattern of perfection, but rather working with her in a reciprocal relationship between equals. If you and I had to wait until whatever we did was excellent before we received praise, we would never be motivated enough to accomplish anything.

When we attend to all eight of these characteristics, applying them with energy and diligence, we will be astounded every day by the difference we can make in the lives of people who have much to learn–ourselves included.

Too Much Time

How, you may ask, are we supposed to accomplish all of these things in the congregate and highly regulated settings in which we offer supports? Haven't we set some very high expectations for ourselves and the persons we support?

First, we need to be sure the setting in which we work (and in which Outsiders have to live) is rich with the media of life, that all the stuff of daily living is not locked away in the interest of safety, efficiency or staff convenience.

Second, we must remember that, in settings designed to help people participate more in their lives, time is our enemy. This is not due to having too little time to accomplish all that must be done. Rather, it is because we rush through chores and meals, taking over household tasks from the people who are rightfully responsible for them, and succumbing to the thinking that we cannot afford to be slowed down by the people we support and teach. Once we finish all of our chores, we find that we have too much time and no meaningful way to fill it. We may then try to come up with meaningful activities for the remaining minutes or hours.

On the other hand, we may feel that there is not enough time to "get everything done." Then, the people we support–and exclude from meaningful tasks–have time on *their* hands. As a result, they may fill that time by engaging in inappropriate behaviors, while we–lacking an appreciation of the result of idle hands–will call in the psychologist to set up a behavior management program. (This adds another task that "takes up all our time.")

MAXIM: *Time is our enemy...because we have too much and no meaningful way to fill it.*

Our answer to the problem of time hanging heavily, on people with a limited repertoire of independent activities, is to take the time to assist them in doing things for themselves. We need to be constantly aware of all the meaningful learning opportunities at their disposal while simply engaging in the tasks of daily living.

TOOLBOX
Making the Use of Time Meaningful

Home Chores. Everyone we serve and support should be given the opportunity to spend time doing chores at home, whether he or she lives in an apartment or shares a room in a "residence with fifty other people." These chores can include such tasks as sweeping the sidewalks, mowing the lawn, washing the dishes (or the car), balancing the checking account, shampooing the carpets, taking out the trash, replacing the batteries in the emergency flashlight–as well as "tooth brushing," "bed making" and "vacuuming."

Home chores increase a person's skills, while also increasing that person's investment in his or her living environment .Involvement in daily chores further improves cooperation with both housemates and support staff. It instills ownership and pride in one's property and home.

Work. Everyone should have the opportunity (indeed, the right) to engage in meaningful work for eight hours a day, five days a week (not "day program" or "vocational activities," but real work, productive tasks that would have to be done if that person weren't doing them). Work has always been the great equalizer for disenfranchised people of all sorts, whether recent immigrants, racial minorities or women. People who work feel good about themselves and are recognized as valuable contributors to society. They earn money that brings them options in how and where to live, options for self-determination. Work empowers.

MAXIM: *Work is a great equalizer. It promotes dignity and respect.*

Dining. Mealtimes should not be a twenty-minute "scarf" and go. They should be rich occasions not just for learning mealtime skills, like using a fork or a napkin, but for developing communication skills, building relationships and savoring the flavors. There is no reason why meals shouldn't be served in three courses with the table cleared between each course. Supper could take two hours, and why not? There's not enough time?

Volunteering. Many of us spend quality time doing volunteer work in our communities. We feel good about ourselves as we share our time, talent and attention. In addition, we build new relationships with people who share our interests. People with disabilities also need to experience being someone who has something to give.

MAXIM: *People with intellectual disabilities have been on the receiving end of giving far too long.*

Leisure. We cherish our leisure time. We love to fill it with events that relax and fulfill us. We like to spend time with our friends, try new activities and see new places. Outsiders, on the other hand, are often relegated to spending their time waiting for something to happen or are forced to participate in meaningless time-fillers, such as going on a van ride.

Home Chores—It's Their Right

Actively participating in home chores:

- **Proclaims this is my home and I am a responsible person**
- **Provides for a meaningful level of engagement**
- **Facilitates the acquisition of new skills**
- **Enhances self-worth**
- **Promotes independence**

Assure that each resident has the opportunity to engage in a minimum of 20 hours of home chores per week.

Free Time

"But what about free time?" you might ask. "It sounds like you want to fill people's every waking hour with tasks from which they can learn. Shouldn't they have time to just kick back and relax?"

The answer is yes, of course they should. There is, however, one caveat: people with disabilities (indeed, all people) have no right to free time in which to engage in inappropriate behavior. They do not need time to shred their shirts, beat their heads against the wall, assault their neighbors or drink themselves into oblivion.

Once again, this maxim does not apply just to people with disabilities. It is relevant to all people who, because of limited options and lack of skill, can find no constructive occupation of their time. It is universal. It applies to elderly people living in nursing homes and young people hanging out on street corners.

> **Free Time**
>
> The people we support have no right to free time...
> to engage in inappropriate behavior.
> Time is our enemy because they have too much of it and
> not a meaningful way to use it.
>
> "Wait" is a vulgar word. What are they waiting for?
> *They are waiting* for lunch.
> *They are waiting* for their medication.
> *They are waiting* to go to their day program.
> *They are waiting* to go to bed.
> *They are waiting* to take a bath.
> *They are waiting* to have a life.
>
> **The amount of free time a person should have is
> determined by their ability to use it.**

MAXIM: *People do not have the right to free time...to engage in inappropriate behavior.*

We do have an obligation–both moral and professional–to help people learn constructive uses of their free time. And we do that the same way we teach any other skill–by providing media, the opportunity, and the assistance and support each person needs to develop his or her competency in making life-enhancing choices for the use of leisure time.

The more competence a person demonstrates, the larger the set of options that can be offered for free time. That set may include just sitting under a tree watching the clouds pass overhead, but not while urinating in his pants. It may include watching television, but not while pinching his neighbor.

People who make an informed choice, from among acceptable options for leisure time, can do virtually anything they want to do in their non-work time. It is our job to support and assist the person in reaching the place where his or her options are not limited by lack of competency, nor by lack of opportunity.

Relationships

If relationships are the task at hand, what kind of media can we use? In the formation of relationships, people are the media. Those of us who work professionally to support and assist people are paid for our relationships. Our task is to make introductions, for example. We help people who have been isolated from the mainstream of society because of their differences to come to know and interact with "the butcher, the baker and the candlestick maker."

Keep in mind the maxim: "If we were all good social workers, we wouldn't need psychologists." Many people consider their interactions with other human beings among the most meaningful events in their lives.

Resistance

I often hear, "Ed doesn't want to do his training program." That communicates to me that some of the Eight Characteristics of Universal Enhancement are missing. Maybe the task is not meaningful to that person. Maybe it is not being scheduled at a time that is appropriate for him or desired by him. It could be that the staff are not participating but are instead standing over the person supervising, doing *to*. Or, there may simply not be sufficient payoff at the end of the task–inadequate compensation. Or, that person may not value the task. So the person being trained asks, rightly, "Why should I bother?"

If training is actually presenting real opportunities for inclusion and participation, there is usually no motivation problem. People want to learn the things that will assist them in developing new relationships and participating in activities that bring them pleasure and joy. People want to learn skills that will free them from the intrusiveness of having others in their space and in their faces providing supports. If we are keeping people from these opportunities, getting them "ready" by teaching them new skills, we have to provide artificial motivation.

If we use the stuff that surrounds real people in real environments as our training equipment, we will soar through skill acquisition and get on to the real task at hand, the development of meaningful relationships.

What if we would all learn and use the eight characteristics of turning supported routines into Universal Enhancement? What if we would ask, show and assist in all our engagements, always striving to avoid doing things alone? What if we would think out loud and take what we can get closest to what we want?

If we acted on these options, the places in which we support and serve people would become places in which all of us grow, develop and increase the quality of our lives (Universal Enhancement), instead of schools where students prepare for some future life that they are told is available when they are "ready."

8

Turning Obstacles Into Opportunities

I sometimes hear objections to implementing the principles and values of Universal Enhancement, and they usually start something like, "Well, that's all a great idea, but we can't because...." The critic then recites a list of reasons why the people served must be dealt with differently from what is proposed in Universal Enhancement. He or she may explain that the people served have dangerous levels of challenging behavior, lack the skills or have serious medical issues. Other reasons include the belief that the community will not accept them, there is not enough money, the surveyors would not like it, the parents do not support it, there is not enough staff...and on and on. Anyone who has worked with Outsiders or disenfranchised persons for any length of time has heard, and probably used, many of the available excuses.

MAXIM: *The reasons you give why it can't be done are the justification for doing it.*

My response is to turn the critic's opposition into a personal challenge. The reasons you give for why it cannot be done are the justification for doing it. At first, this appears to be a facile rejoinder, but if we look more deeply, we see that it is a guide to help us balance the sometimes conflicting demands of opportunity and protection.

Let us start with a simple example. Why is there no salt shaker on the dining room table at suppertime? The reason given is that Susie is on a diet prescribed by her physician that prohibits added salt. That is exactly why the salt has to be there–so Susie can learn that she needs to use the salt substitute. Susie should be given support and assistance as she learns how to choose for herself, but no more help than she truly needs. Transitional support is merely being provided along the way as Susie learns to run her own life.

Why is Joe not allowed to go to the mall? Because the last time he was there, he "pitched a fit," broke a planter and scared a lot of shoppers. Well, that is why he needs to go on the next trip–so we can help him learn how to shop appropriately at the mall. Offer Joe the opportunity of shopping at the mall, while at the same time assuring that his disruptive and socially inappropriate behaviors are redirected. Help him by providing the supports, assistance and guidance he needs for having an enjoyable and successful shopping trip.

Why does Terry have no key to his house? The reason given is that he will lose or swallow it. Well, how is he ever going to learn to use a key if he has no opportunity to have one until he knows how to use it? We need to accept the challenge to identify and apply creative supports for Terry, so he can have the key to

Front Door Key

Having a key to your front door proclaims ownership and control his house. We may want to help Terry purchase a key chain (like the ones staff members wear). We may decide to help Terry put his key on a plastic paddle device to prevent him from losing or swallowing it (like the kind used at the corner gas station to keep people from putting the restroom keys in their pockets). Or we may need to carry Terry's key for him temporarily, handing it to him as we approach the door. And, we may need to assist him with placing it in the lock, unlocking the door and returning the key to us for safekeeping. What is clear is that Terry's quality of life is not enhanced by accepting his inappropriate or skill-deficient behavior as a justification for denying him a key to his house.

Reasonable Risks: A Question of Balance

Recall the characteristics of the institution, in particular the denial of the dignity that results from the opportunity to engage in risky and challenging endeavors. As children, most of us learned important as well as trivial tasks by being allowed, by parents or caretakers, to take reasonable risks. This was done in order to give us the opportunity to develop the skills and understanding that would allow us to rise to a new occasion.

Of course, our parents filtered those risks, not allowing us, for instance, to play in the street for the opportunity of learning about speeding cars. In such a case, the consequences for not having learned the lesson are too dire. Likewise, I do not advocate that you put gasoline in a pitcher on the dining room table, so that Susie can learn not to drink it. But the salt that is not allowed in Susie's salt-free diet will not cause her to drop dead at the dinner table. We, and Susie, must be willing to allow her the potential risk of getting some salt, in order to allow her the opportunity to learn how to control her own salt intake. If Susie is denied this opportunity to participate in and control what at first glance is a trivial element of her own life, she may thereby also be denied the opportunity to eat in a restaurant with her family or go to a friend's house for dinner. She may never be allowed to go places where salt is likely to be on the table.

Helping a person you support to choose which risks are "reasonable" and which are unacceptably dangerous is an exacting job. As risk assessors (another form of Gatekeeper), we are like Lady Justice, blindfolded, a balance scale held out in front of us. On one arm of the scale is opportunity/risk; on the other is protection. Seeking the right proportion of each element is a tricky task indeed. If we come down too far in one direction, we may face charges of carelessness because a person's life may be endangered. If we come down too far the other way, we stifle the growth of the people we serve and deny them the right to have a life.

Parents whose children live with them usually know their children's abilities well enough to assess which risks are permissible. But, many of us know of parents who err on the conservative side; we call them overprotective. And, we know of those whose mistaken judgments fall on the overly-lenient side; we call them negligent. The same categories can be applied to people who offer supports and assistance to Outsiders.

An important point to bear in mind here is that the assessment of the reasonableness of a particular risk should not be based on the perceived abilities or disabilities of the people we support. It should be based on *our own ability or inability* to provide the needed assistance, protective oversight or environmental safeguards. Seen in this light, the assessment process takes on a whole different aspect. The process includes an assessment of the environment, adaptations that may be needed, and an evaluation of resources available (including people resources) to support a person.

Our assessment knowledge also needs to include an understanding of the unique characteristics of the individual for whom we will be providing support. For instance, deciding whether it is an acceptable risk for Susie to have a salt shaker on her dinner table depends on our assessment of whether or not we can give Susie the supervision she needs for success and safety. Joe's response at the mall is another example. He may have reacted disruptively because he does not like to be around large crowds of people. Many of us have similar dislikes or discomforts as evidenced by increased anxiety around crowded holiday shopping venues. An alternative may be to go at less busy, hectic times.

Professionals, family members and friends who have accepted the responsibility of assisting people to achieve their highest levels of freedom and independence are held accountable for making decisions about the minimum level of support a particular individual needs in a particular situation. Most of the professionally designed and marketed assessment devices provide little assistance or direction in this crucial task. Nor will the regulations that guide much of our behavior provide us with the necessary judgments. The regulations are designed for the protection of categorical masses of people seen as needing to be safeguarded–elders, children and people with disabilities. No regulation can help us respond to the idiosyncrasies, sensitivities, hopes and desires of the myriad individuals we serve.

Turning Obstacles into Opportunities

I have found, in actual practice, that if we will think of every objection as an opportunity for learning and a challenge to be overcome, we can turn obstacles into opportunities. This kind of challenge keeps us on our toes, keeps us from sanitizing environments to the point where there is not enough real media, the "stuff" of which real life is constructed. In addition, it keeps us away from the extreme "rightist" position, the stance of the supposed advocate who is so concerned with the rights and freedoms of the person with disabilities that the right to be free from harm takes a back seat.

TALE

I recently visited a small rest home for the purpose of meeting someone who was considering moving into a new home where supports and services would be provided. As I neared the home, I passed a young man standing on the double yellow line of the exit ramp, gesturing to passing vehicles that he wanted a cigarette. He was clearly in danger. The road

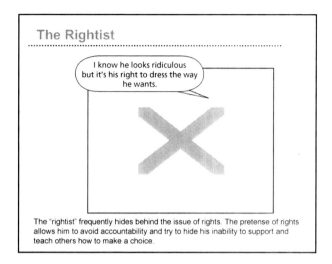

was remote from any dwellings other than the place I was visiting. When I arrived, I asked the rest home's director about the young man.

"Oh, he stays there all the time," said the director.

"But isn't it dangerous?" I asked.

"Of course, it is," he replied, "but it's his right to be there."

I disagree strenuously with the director's position. More in line with the concepts of Universal Enhancement would be to provide the opportunity to learn other ways of obtaining cigarettes and interacting with people. There was neither dignity nor opportunity in this kind of foolish risk-taking. One's rights should not be unnecessarily restricted, but failure to protect from harm or permitting/supporting a person to take unnecessary risks may be regarded as neglect.

Hierarchy of Responsibility

While there is no list of acceptable and unacceptable risks, some direction can be provided. We can use the Trilogy of Service Principles introduced in Chapter 3.

1. Protect from harm
2. Assure dignity and respect
3. Provide learning opportunities

If any of these responsibilities comes into conflict with another, the one with the higher position on the list takes precedence. Thus, we sometimes find ourselves forgoing dignity and respect temporarily in the interest of protecting a person from harm. For example, we may use a personal restraint or restrictive device to prevent a person from injuring himself. (While not very dignified, we try to apply them with respect.) But, we will not sacrifice this person's dignity or the respect we have for him in order to achieve some habilitative goal (that is, to teach new skills). It does not matter how noble the educational endeavor may seem.

So, does making protection from harm the highest obligation perpetuate the problem in the Medical/Custodial Model, where the doctors and nurses did not let anyone do anything because they were afraid someone might get hurt? The answer lies in a careful definition of protection from harm (also known as protective oversight).

Harm, in this instance, means that a person would incur substantial injury or damage, physical or emotional, that would take some effort to repair. The focus is not on protecting someone from the reasonable woes and embarrassments of everyday life–the skinned knees, the hurt feelings, the disappointment arising from a failed relationship, or the frustration of not always getting what you want. That sort of excessive concern would indeed lead to the overprotective attitude

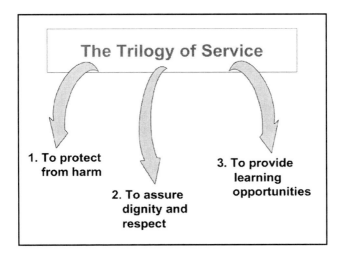

that causes people to coddle and shelter people who seem unable to negotiate the world on their own. The concern is not only with freedom from harmful, dangerous or uncomfortable circumstances, but also with freedom to be an active participant in life.

When we are wrestling with these decisions, it may help to keep in mind the kind of criteria we use in deciding what opportunities to allow ourselves. The risks are weighed against the benefits. If the risk includes a good possibility of real harm, we assess the benefits we would receive from engaging in the activity. When the benefits outweigh the risks, we generally go ahead. This is called enlightened risk. For instance, if a man decides that the imagined benefits of cross-country skiing do not outweigh the risk that his heart condition could cause a severe medical emergency in a remote area, he will abstain. We call this prudence.

It is important to note that the element of enlightenment poses a burden. As professionals, who are paid to provide supervision for a person deemed incapable of making certain judgments, or as a family member or friend who has assumed some of this responsibility, our burden is to weigh both risks and benefits and come to a prudent decision for *someone else*. With this responsibility, we do not allow the person with limited judgment of risk to engage in possibly fatal or damaging activities for the sake of a momentary rush of pleasure.

We do not, interestingly enough, deny ourselves such a rush. Normatives are required to be neither prudent nor reasonable. If we want to engage in bungee jumping, hang gliding, or casual sex because we derive some enormous perceived benefit from these activities, we are allowed to choose to do so even though they all carry a substantial, and possibly fatal, risk.

We probably will, however, assist the persons we support to choose activities that may have a high risk but nevertheless carry a significant and ongoing benefit. Some examples are riding in an automobile, flying in a commercial airplane, and living in a high-rise apartment building. These activities, though risky, open up worlds of opportunity for a person, and most of us consider the benefits to be worth the risks.

At the next level of the hierarchy, we will not do anything in the name of learning opportunities that diminishes our obligation to treat the persons we serve with dignity and respect. We will not talk to them in a harsh or demeaning way because "they have to learn to listen." We will not subject a person to meaningless, repetitive tasks that none of us would do for five minutes just because "it's part of her training program." We will not barge into the bathroom because "we need to keep a record on the BM chart." We will seek to offer people the opportunity to learn new skills, but not at the expense of losing their dignity or self-respect.

Teaching Self-Determination: Choice and Decision Making

The Trilogy of Service Principles gives us some guidance in knowing how to support people in setting their priorities. But, how can we contribute most effectively to their learning to make decisions for themselves? In our day-to-day working with Outsiders, what choices and options are appropriate?

The answer is that we start with a limited set of options and expand the size of that set as the person demonstrates the skills needed to handle more complex decision-making tasks.

MAXIM: *The more capable a person is, the larger the set of options he or she is offered.*

For example, to help a man with intellectual disabilities who requires pervasive supports choose the clothes he wants to wear to work that day, you would probably not just open his closet and say, "Max, what do you want to wear to work today?" If you did, Max might answer that he wishes to wear the lime green shorts and the lavender T-shirt.

On this day, if the forecast calls for a high temperature of thirty degrees with a good chance of freezing rain, you might, instead, offer a choice of two shirts. Both are appropriate for the weather and for

Max's work activities, so you ask, "Which shirt do you want to wear today, Max? The blue one or the green one?"

Max may make no response, and you may have to help him by lifting his hand and supporting it to touch one of the shirts. But then you will compliment Max for the good choice he made and go on to support Max in choosing a pair of pants from a set that contains two pairs appropriate to the season and the activity.

With this method, you have successfully met the challenge of *reason giving* (excuses for not doing something) by making it the *justification* for addressing the problem or issue. You once thought, "Max can't pick out his own clothes. He always picks the wrong colors, and he wants to wear his wool shirt in the summertime." But now, you have moved in a creative direction, recognizing that Max's apparent inability to choose appropriate clothes is exactly the justification for the necessity of helping him make a choice.

As Max's ability to choose increases, you will provide him with more items from which to choose, eventually even including that wool shirt on a summer day. But this time, because you have limited the options for Max, he may have come to know that he will be a lot more comfortable at work if he chooses a T-shirt. Limiting options is not a denial of rights when it is in support of the right to learn how to make decisions, the right of self-determination.

MAXIM: *Don't give people choices; teach them to make them.*

Normatives may be involved in a similar process when we have to make decisions in an arena where we have limited competence or experience. For example, if a couple is decorating their living room and do not have much color sense, they may hire an interior decorator to present them with a manageable set of options. She probably would not just turn them loose to choose the colors for the curtains. She would say, "Your sofa is blue, and those chairs are green. Here are some colors I think would go well with the furniture." Then, she would offer them a limited set of options, each of which could be successful. The couple would be learning to choose colors by being guided by someone who has more experience than they do. The same process holds true for Outsiders. Do not just give people choices; teach them to make them.

TALE
Young Dudes Support Choice...and Tom Learns a Lesson

One morning, I visited a home in North Dakota at 6:30 a.m. When I knocked on the door, a very young male employee opened it. I was admittedly prejudiced by this young man's appearance. He was wearing a baseball cap (backwards), and I have some negative feelings about people wearing caps in the house. I looked at his pants and saw a tear in the right knee. I thought, "This is going to be a disaster." Here was a young man who apparently had not worked at the home very long and who obviously did not know how to present himself in a very favorable light. In my mind, I called him "Dude."

I went inside. The home was unusually quiet. There were four women living there, and all of them used wheelchairs for mobility.

I intended to be an unobtrusive observer, so I quietly walked into the dining room where the four women were sitting around a table. Another young man in garb similar to Dude's was standing near the table. He had several days unshaven beard growth, further increasing my anxiety. I began to think of him as "Beard."

As I watched, Dude approached one of the women and said, "Susan, can I help you go to the kitchen, and we'll get some cereal and bring it back to the table?"

Well, the way that man talked to Susan immediately got my attention. He spoke no louder than was necessary for Susan to hear. He spoke with courtesy and respect. I was impressed. Then, while guiding her hands as necessary, he helped Susan release the brakes of her wheelchair. They went slowly into the kitchen.

The cereal was in a cabinet that was not accessible to a person using a wheelchair. Dude opened the cabinet and said, "Hey, let's get some of these cereals into the dining room." He brought a box of Cheerios halfway down from the cabinet and then assisted Susan in taking the Cheerios the rest of the way down to the tray on her wheelchair. Then, he brought down a box of Grape-Nuts and corn flakes in the same fashion. Finally, he asked Susan if he could help her return to the dining room.

When they got back to the dining room table, Dude helped Susan relock her wheelchair brakes, while Beard walked around the table, quietly assisting the other women.

Dude continued working with Susan. "May I help you give the cereal to Linda, so she can decide which one she wants for breakfast?" he asked her politely.

He helped Susan place each box in a row in front of Linda. Beard came up behind Linda and asked, "Which cereal would you like this morning, Linda?"

Linda took in the row of cereal boxes with an apparently vacant gaze. Then she looked up at Beard and back at the cereal. Suddenly, she thrust her arm out and knocked over the box of Cheerios.

Beard seized the occasion and said, "Oh, you'd like Cheerios this morning. May I help you pour some?"

MAXIM: *Speak no louder than necessary for the person to whom you are speaking to hear you.*

Well, it was obvious to me by now that these two gentlemen fully understood what they were doing. They realized the importance of offering options to support choice making, and they had the personal resources that allowed them to treat those women with the dignity and respect they deserved.

It was I who had fallen short, judging these men by stereotyping them based on my first impression. I should have known better, and I learned much from those young men that cold Dakota morning.

Relationships and Choice

When encouraging and supporting people to make choices in more important and complex life areas than what clothes to wear, the application of the principle of enlightened risk becomes more difficult. We may be forced to make careful judgments about risk factors, benefits and a person's current abilities.

For individuals under the aegis of a service system, risk/opportunity decisions are usually based on assessments and goals we have set at some kind of annual planning meeting. There we gather a team of people, so that we can pool our resources and perspectives, in order to make decisions based on enlightened risk. It is a pretty efficient process (and, incidentally, spreads the liability so that no individual gets the blame for a faulty decision), but there is no way we can really get to know a new person in the thirty days we usually have prior to a "staffing." No matter how many professional assessments we administered, how many test scores we accumulated, it would be like trying to buy a meaningful birthday present for someone you just read about in the newspaper, a person you only met once.

This is the crux of the issue. Assessing the balance of risks and benefits and deciding on appropriate sets from which to encourage choice making depends on *relationship*. It depends on knowing something about the person, recognizing that no human being is a barrel with limited capacity, and believing deeply that unless that person has an opportunity to take a risk, he or she will never learn anything.

This kind of relationship–truly knowing a person–develops more often with friends, relatives and the people who provide direct support and assistance than it does with professionals who have merely administered standardized assessment devices. We may ask, "Do you think Lawrence would like to learn to walk to the store?" The person who works with Lawrence every day, or the friend or family member who has a close relationship with him, is more on the mark saying, "Yeah, I think he'd love to do that, and I think he could do it." On the other hand, the professional who has *assessed* Lawrence may indicate that he is "not ready" yet.

Relationships, opportunities, choices–these are the essential elements of an environment in which people can grow, learn and become more independent. And these are the cornerstones of Universal Enhancement.

9

"Because We're Not Children Anymore"

Before a final discussion of the elements of Universal Enhancement, a vital issue must be addressed. This issue frequently raises significant emotional reaction because, unfortunately, it goes to the root of our perceptions about a person with intellectual disabilities and other people who have been disenfranchised. It is the tendency to treat those we believe to be inferior to us as children.

This infantilizing of those considered as Outsiders, persons not worthy of the respect and courtesy usually accorded adults, pervades nearly all areas that concern people viewed as unequal. The issue arises when African-American adult males are referred to as "Boy," when a seventy-year-old woman is called "Sweetie," or when migrant workers are seen as happy campers. It arises anytime adults are treated as children. Professionals in the field of disabilities services have come to call the issue *age appropriateness*.

Who Is an Adult?

This discussion will begin with a definition that seems almost too obvious to warrant consideration. What constitutes an adult? The answer is simple: adulthood is determined by how long you have lived, not by IQ, physical prowess, academic competence or life-skills ability. If you are eighteen (or twenty-one) years old, you are an adult–period.

People who lack those abilities and skills you would expect them to have, given their years of life experience, are not "children in adult bodies." Nor are they "just like little kids." They are adults who have both strengths/abilities in some areas and skill deficits in other areas, which require certain levels of support and assistance in some of their life activities. In this need for support and assistance, they are no different from Normatives. We all require some degree of support and help in many areas of our lives. Thus, none of us is truly independent; we are all interdependent.

MAXIM: *Adulthood is determined only by age.*

Nothing points up this interdependence more than the large number of specialists in our society who help us with the complicated tasks we do not know how to do, or just do not care to do. For instance, I used to change the oil in my car. It was a mark of independence for me to take care of my own needs. Recently, I have started turning the job over to the Fast Way Oil Change down the street. (Their motto is "Let us do your dirty work!") I have not lost any of my manly status by allowing the guys at Fast Way to change the oil. I am not a child because I rely on others for support and assistance. And, the Fast Way employees earn their living serving customers in a quick and efficient manner. Fast Way guys and I are now interdependent, an enhancement for both parties.

MAXIM: *None of us are independent; we are all interdependent.*

The prejudicial notion that people who lack certain abilities are like children is commonly applied to persons who have been demeaned and cast aside because they are not capable, competent and independent (as all of us imagine ourselves to be). It is not uncommon to hear someone talk to an adult with blindness as if he had to have things spelled out for him simply, the way you would talk to a five-year-old child. Or, a well-meaning neighbor might talk to an eighty-five-year-old woman as if she had just arrived on the planet and needed the patronizing patience offered to a creature who is unfamiliar with our culture or language. The notion that adulthood is somehow linked with competence, independence or normalcy for a certain age is often so deeply ingrained that it is no wonder the least competent people among us receive the most condescending treatment.

"But We Love Children"

Many people have never taken the time to process their feelings about this issue of treating adult Outsiders like children. If you are a friend, family member, or support person of someone who has disabilities and you really care about them, you may already be asking, "Well, what's wrong with seeing these people as children? I love children, just as I love the person to whom I provide services and support. Being treated as a child is a wonderful life experience. Children are protected from the unpleasantness of life. Children are doted upon and cared for. The life of a child is a wonderful life."

Most people would agree with this sentiment. We do, after all, love and cherish our children. We care for them, keep them safe and help them with the things they are unable to do for themselves. When this attitude is applied, however, to aging parents who require nursing services, to adult sons or daughters who have developmental disabilities or to migrant farm workers, we begin to see that being treated as a child, when one is, in fact, an adult, is usually demeaning, disrespectful and limiting. In most cultures, we do not–and this is critically important–extend to children the same courtesy, respect and opportunity we unhesitatingly offer to adults.

Respect and opportunity–these are the crucial factors.

Privacy

Let's look at an example of the issue of privacy. Many mothers have no qualms about taking their newly toilet-trained little boys into the women's restroom with them. Many fathers have no problem changing their one-year-old daughter's diapers on a picnic table at the public park. But, what would our reaction be were a family member to assist a forty-year-old woman with her toileting needs in public? Does such a display become acceptable because the woman has the abilities of a one-year-old, which is to say that she lacks most of the competencies you would expect to see in a woman her age?

Lack of Privacy

In our society, adults are expected to maintain and receive a greater level of personal privacy than that required of children. An adult who does not protect his own privacy, because he has never been taught to be private or to respect the privacy of others, may be shunned as unsocialized, odd and somehow threatening. Carla, a two-year-old girl who comes into the living room while her father's assembled friends are playing poker and offers to show an adult acquaintance her new panties is considered cute. Lily, a woman of thirty with intellectual disabilities who does the same thing, is seen as lewd or, even worse, embarrassing, placing her outside accepted social conventions and mores.

It is crucial that we understand the chain of events here. Some might see Lily as a child in an adult body because she lacks the judgment and ability of the normative woman her age. Those who see her as a child are likely to habitually support behavior that is acceptable in children. Since Lily has not been offered the opportunity to learn adult behavior, she acts like a child. Because she acts like a child, she is perceived as a child. Lily is caught in a circular trap of our construction. And, it is we who must help her escape.

Opportunity

More impacting than the issue of privacy is the matter of opportunity. We do not offer to children the same opportunities for involvement in the community, participation in activities, choice and decision making, and wide access to initiating relationships that we extend to adults. We justify limiting our children's opportunities because, as their concerned guardians, we deem some of them too risky. As they demonstrate more competence in an area, we offer children more options, even some than they are not ready for. That is, we offer them the opportunity to try new things, even though they may possibly fail.

We usually make our decisions about the type of opportunity that we extend by considering the child's age. We expect a four-year-old to be able to stay overnight at Uncle George's house or a fourteen-year-old to be old enough to go out on a date with a group of her peers. The child may not have demonstrated the requisite competencies for the challenging activity, but we make a judgment based on what we know about her and the expectations we have of what a similar-aged child is likely to be able to do.

MAXIM: *There is no regulation for having a life.*

Now apply this principle to Sam, age fifty-two, who has an IQ of fifty-eight. Which influences our expectations for Sam more, his IQ score or his age? Sam is single and has no family responsibilities. He works as a janitor at a shoe store four hours a day, earning a sub-minimum wage that was arranged by his job coach. He lives in a group home with five other men who also have intellectual disabilities.

On Monday night, Sam expresses an interest in going down to the Blue Ribbon Bar and Grill to drink a few beers and watch a football game with some of his coworkers from the store. The staff at the group home are very surprised at this request because they regard Sam as a ten-year-old boy in a gray-headed body. The issues they see as important for Sam's growth and development are his immaturity and lack of social skills.

For instance, just last night at dinner, Sam had a tantrum after the staff refused to let him take his Ninja Turtles coloring book, which he carries all the time, to the dinner table. The staff have been teaching Sam that we do not take our toys to the dinner table. Since they perceive Sam as a person with childish desires and behaviors, no one who provides supports for him has ever considered the possibility that he might wish to go to a bar and hang out with men his own age. How could they have? The staff are working on the lessons that children need to learn: "Don't bring your toys to the table." They are not helping Sam develop a repertoire of adult skills, activities and opportunities that will bring a level of successful participation into his life.

Clearly, the staff who work at Sam's home perceived and treated him as a child because he has an IQ of fifty-eight, indicating that he requires intermittent and/or continuous support. They will be able to offer him the opportunities and alternatives typically available to a man his age only if they are able to see beyond their limited perspective. Then, they can remove the shackles from his life, and allow him to explore new interests and relationships that will carry him far beyond a life devoted to a coloring book.

Offering Alternatives

Now is when the "rightist" frequently speaks up and proclaims, in pained disbelief, "Do you mean they should take Sam's coloring book away from him?" The answer is always no. Only a fool would take things away from people. Taking something away from someone is neither an alternative nor a solution.

When people are offered appropriate options, they are more likely to choose objects and activities that will enhance their acceptance and, thus, bring them more opportunities for participation and relationships. Unless held back by some external force, most people yearn for the greater range of options and increased freedom that come with adulthood. It is a natural tendency, common to people all over the world, to "put away childish things."

MAXIM: *Only a fool would take things away from people.*

Thus, there is no reason to take away items and events that are not age appropriate, because an adult with adult opportunities will seldom choose the limitations imposed by childish things. He or she will more likely choose the increased range of choice making and personal autonomy brought about by participation in age-appropriate activities with age peers. (Note that some of us may choose to

collect toys or wear cartoon character T-shirts, but because we have competence, people are not likely to see those things as childish.)

Instead, Sam can be offered more alternatives. Then, if he does choose to sit in his room holding his coloring book, it is not because he did not know that he could also choose to go down to the Blue Ribbon on Monday night to watch the game or walk to the park to pitch horseshoes with other men his age.

Critics may respond that participation in adult activities is unrealistic for a person with severe disabilities. It is certainly unrealistic to expect that Sam will become a rocket scientist or president of the United States; but it is definitely not unrealistic to expect him to have the opportunity to have a full, adult life of his choosing.

MAXIM: *"Special" is a code word for segregation.* ™

Professional habilitators are often so bound by systems of goals, plans and training programs that they fail to see the wonderful training opportunities available through participation in everyday adult activities. For instance, staff may keep Sam from going to the bar to watch the game because he has to stay home and work on his leisure

> **Having a Life**
>
> There are no regulatory requirements for supporting a person in getting a life. When was the last time you were "cited" because persons receiving support...
>
> Tag 5.30 – Were not missed when they were away.
>
> Tag 3.21 – Had no one to send them a birthday card.
>
> Tag 2.42 – Were not taught how to whistle or snap their fingers.
>
> Tag 5.51 – Were not smiling.
>
> Tag 4.63 – Were not told how "handsome" or "pretty" they looked when all dressed up for church.
>
> Tag 3.22 – Were not encouraged to make a snowman on the day of the first big snow.
>
> Tag 3.85 – Were not greeted by support staff with a warm "How are you today?"
>
> Tag 9.37 – Were denied an opportunity for a consensual sexual relationship.

skills training program. Or, they may fail to appreciate that by playing horseshoes with his buddies at the park, Sam will learn social skills–turn-taking, standing in line and eye-hand coordination–while also developing relationships and having fun (an activity which is usually not included in the program plan).

TALE
The Great Playground Massacre

People who attempt to alter environments in conformance to contemporary standards of age appropriateness are often rejected and scorned, like the prophet who is "without honor in his own country."

When I took a position as assistant superintendent at a large state-run facility, charged with the responsibility of implementing the kinds of principles espoused in Universal Enhancement, I set out to make some changes that were popular neither with the staff nor with the families of the people who lived there.

One obvious problem was that immediately adjacent to a living area occupied only by adults was a child's playground. I would ride past it on my way to the administration building and see forty-three-year-old men sliding down the sliding board and fifty-year-old women riding the rocking snail. Sometimes, two gray-haired "toddlers" sat together digging holes in the sandbox.

Finally, it was too much for me. I felt indignant when I observed people older than me, people who should be experiencing dignity and respect, engaged in childish activities that seemed demeaning to me. They had a right to be offered options—options that were more age appropriate. So I met with a number of the residents of the institution and discussed with them what alternative recreation and relaxation items they might be interested in having on the campus grounds. The residents made many excellent recommendations. I gave the orders, and big changes were made.

The next morning, workmen arrived and removed the sliding boards, jungle gyms, merry-go-rounds and Dumbo swings. In their place, a new park started to take shape. It was a park for adults—park benches, basketball courts, horseshoe pits, curved walks with nice landscaping, porch type glides, outdoor tables and chairs for playing board games or just sipping an al fresco cup of coffee.

The staff was livid. They felt their playground had been destroyed. They convened a meeting of residents and staff and called me before this tribunal to defend my actions. I listened quietly as one staff person after another made the case that the residents' rights had been violated, that they had lost something precious, that the people who lived in that unit loved those Dumbo swings.

Finally, one of the women who lived at the institution, a frail, elderly woman sitting in a wheelchair near the back of the room, raised her hand. She was recognized to speak, and the roomful of people fell silent as they strained to hear her soft voice.

"I think I know why he did it," she said, and stopped for a breath. "He took out the little kids' toys, because...we're not children anymore."

The silence that followed lasted a long time.

I finally found my voice and said, "That's right; you're not children anymore. And now that you're truly adults, you'll never be treated like children again."

No one is likely to offer adult opportunities to children. If we see people with intellectual disabilities, elderly people or people with physical impairments as children, treat them as children, and surround them with the images of childhood, they will likely fulfill our prophecy and act like children. They will not have the opportunity to experience risk, love, autonomy or any of the things we looked forward to when, as children, we dreamed of being grown-ups.

R-E-S-P-E-C-T

Respect is another prerogative of adulthood. Unfortunately, children in our society are generally not accorded the same respect and courtesy as adults. One could certainly make the case that children, as human beings, are entitled to that respect, but we often couple respect with competence, a highly regarded quality in our modern Western culture. We respect people who have proven themselves through their accomplishments, abilities and performance. Those among us whose capabilities fall below the normative threshold, usually through no fault of their own, often become the targets of disrespect. It is no prize to be considered childish.

It is likely that people who do not know our friend Sam will not offer him the respect usually given a man of his age if they see him carrying the child's coloring book. Once again, the self-fulfilling prophecy rears its ugly head. And, what happens to people who do not receive respect? They do not give it, either. They become Outsiders, and their failure to demonstrate respect justifies their outsider status. They are caught in a vicious cycle. Can anyone be surprised that the woman who is treated like a child is on a training program to reduce tantrums?

Doing "Stupid" Things

Already mentioned briefly, alcohol use is a hot human rights issues that is largely affected by our attitudes toward age appropriateness. It is only one of the many health and safety concerns that impose one standard for adults and another for children. Just as we do not let children drink alcohol, we also do not let them use tobacco or engage in sexual intercourse. We do not let them eat too much junk food, nor do we let them get involved in relationships we think might harm them.

Similar judgments are made about adult behavior. Most of us believe that adults who act wisely use alcohol in moderation, avoid tobacco use, eat a sensible diet and develop relationships with decent people. On the other hand, behaving stupidly includes drunkenness, chain smoking, compulsive eating and promiscuity. Being responsible caretakers of our own offspring, we feel obligated to keep them from engaging in stupid behavior.

However, the fact that there are no laws prohibiting excessive or unhealthy behavior in adults demonstrates our general societal belief

---

RESPECT

Responsive
Encouraging
Sensitive
Perceptive
Expediting
Caring
Thoughtful

It must start with respecting yourself.

that adults have the right to do stupid things–unless, that is, the adult has not passed the Gatekeepers' competency test. Outsiders lose the opportunity to make stupid adult choices. Instead, they continue to live under the double standard that supports our making protective decisions for children.

We decide tobacco use is a health risk and, therefore, Walter (IQ 65) should be weaned off his chewing tobacco. But, we establish policies for where and when staff can smoke outside Walter's home. We decide Sheila (IQ 61) is not ready to go on a date with the man she met at the workshop. But, we rearrange the staff schedule because Yvonne (IQ 98), who was recently hired to work nights, had a rough morning dealing with her abusive husband and did not show up for work.

We put Joe (IQ 24) on a fifteen-hundred-calorie diet because he is ten pounds over his ideal body weight, while Zeke (IQ 117) goes on medical leave for the heart attack brought about by his high cholesterol and high blood pressure. Once again, the point is that being an adult is determined by age and not by IQ (or any other test of competence). People who are adults should have the opportunities that adults have, including the opportunity to do stupid things, the opportunity to fail.

This is not to say that people with disabilities should use alcohol or tobacco, eat themselves into obesity, or enter into abusive relationships (for the same reasons we do not advocate these behaviors for Normatives). But, if we assist the person we support to develop an understanding of both the range of options available and of the consequences that go with each option, his ability to make reasonably informed decisions is enhanced.

As described earlier, we accomplish this by balancing the risk with the opportunity. We can start by examining the ways a person served is being treated like a child, and looking instead for a similar opportunity that is available only to adults. Thus, instead of encouraging Sam to color in his childish coloring book, we assist him to pursue an art class at the local community center.

We heard a story (told by Lynne Seagle of Hope House Foundation in Norfolk, Virginia) of a man with intellectual disabilities who had recently moved out of a group home into his own home. (The move highlights the fact that "group home" may be an oxymoron). His mother had left him a small trust fund when she died, and it was this money that he used, supervised by his aunt, to maintain the house in which he lived. One day, the staff who supported him could not find him and discovered that his trust fund money was missing, too.

A week later, he returned, broke. He had run off with a stripper he had met in a bar, and she had helped him spend his savings before she disappeared. The agency staff were upset with him for having been so irresponsible. His reply was, "It was the best date I ever had." Now, who are we to say that that man should not have had the opportunity to blow his savings on the best date he ever had? Would we want someone breathing down our necks, constantly monitoring to make sure we always made smart decisions? Of course not. Why should it be any different for people with disabilities?

MAXIM: *When given options, people tend to choose those things that enhance their dignity and respect.* ™

It is important to be mindful of the special obligations and responsibilities taken on by agencies that operate under contractual oversight demands (See Chapter 5.). The challenge faced by such organizations is to offer and encourage bounded options—neither supporting the "anything goes" attitude of total license, nor succumbing to the "nothing doing" stance of the institution. From an organizational and professional perspective, we have a covenant with those we support: to do them no harm.

A great deal of space has been devoted to the issue of age appropriateness because it is crucial to the final step in Universal Enhancement, inclusion in the community. If we see people with competence limitations as children, we will not allow them the opportunities to take risks and explore the world in which they live. We will continue to keep them sheltered and not allow them to participate in the communities in which they live. They will not be afforded the same opportunities we cherish and demand as adults, so they will never be able to live full lives–lives replete with both success and failure, with smart decisions as well as stupid ones.

No one told us we had to be perfect in order to be treated as adults. Let's not hold a double standard for people who have failed some kind of test of acceptance.

TALE
Trick or Treat

I was conducting a presentation one early October for an agency that provided residential and habilitation services to people with disabilities. While I was talking about age appropriateness, I noticed an older woman in the audience who seemed extremely distressed.

Having occasionally listened to parents argue the case for continuing to treat their adult offspring as children, I assumed I knew why the woman was upset. Perhaps she thought I was advocating taking an age inappropriate item away from her son or daughter, something the mother felt was necessary to show that she cared for her "handicapped child."

When it was time for a break, the woman remained in her seat, apparently deep in thought. I asked one of my hosts who she was.

The man replied, "Oh, she's a member of our board of directors, and she has a son who has Down syndrome."

"How old is her son?" I asked.

"I think he's about thirty-five," the host replied. "He attends our sheltered workshop."

This information bore out my initial appraisal. Just as I was about to head for the refreshment table, the woman approached me, a deep frown furrowing her brow, the trace of a tear on her cheek.

"Dr. Pomeranz," she said, "can I speak with you a minute?"

Here it comes, I thought: "I love my child. He's my baby, and he'll always be my baby. Why can't he sit on the floor and play with his rubber ducky? He needs to be protected." This was the all-too-frequently-heard parental objection to treating adults as adults.

"Sure," I said. "What's on your mind?"

"Well," said the woman, pausing for breath, "I've been thinking about what you were saying, and I've come to a decision. I'd like to share it with you." She paused again to compose her words.

"You know that Halloween is coming up. Well, my decision is that this will be the first time in thirty years that I'm not going to dress my son up in a clown costume and parade him up and down the street trick-or-treating." Her voice broke a little. I could see that this was a difficult and significant moment for her.

"What do you think your son would like to do instead?" I asked.

"I think," she replied, "he'd like to stay home and help pass out the candy to the kids who come to the door."

TOOLBOX
Making the Use of Time Meaningful

Sometimes, it is a real challenge to identify training and leisure items that are appropriate to a person's age but do not challenge too greatly his or her degree of competence. We must be creative to meet that challenge. For example, items do not have to be used in the way they were intended for a person to enjoy interacting with them. Following are some ideas.

Puzzles

Adults play with puzzles, but the typical five hundred-piece jigsaw puzzle is too difficult for some people. The alternative ten-piece puzzle is usually a picture of Barney or Rainbow Brite or some other subject that is suitable for a five-year-old but not a fifty-year-old.

A simple solution is to make your own puzzle. Assist the person in selecting and purchasing a vinyl placemat with a typical landscape scene of boats in a harbor, autumn leaves or ocean waves–scenes that interest the puzzlemaker. Set the placemat on a hard surface with the picture face down. With a felt-tipped pen, divide it into six segments (or fewer, depending on the person's ability). Cut along the lines, turn the pieces back over and *voila!* You have a six-piece puzzle. If the puzzle master gets good at this one, cut the pieces in half–a twelve-piece puzzle!

Coloring Books

Many adults like to draw and paint. Sometimes a person, who has limited competence, is only offered coloring books and crayons. However, most coloring books are made for children; they feature clowns, puppy dogs and cartoon characters. And, most adults have not used wax crayons in years.

Instead, help the person buy a tablet of blank drawing paper and colorful pencils or felt-tipped markers. This "artist's pad" and other media can indulge any penchant for graphic expression.

Games

Many adult board games require reading skills and the ability to develop complex strategies. But some do not.

UNO® is a card game often played by groups of people that include those who have disabilities. It is fun, fast and simple. If you can match colors, you can play.

Bingo is another easy board game played by adults. Try to avoid "picture" Bingo. The pictures are usually very childish.

Jenga® (also known as Ta-Ka-Ra-Di) is a game of stacking small blocks. It helps develop strategic thinking and fine motor skills– and not a cartoon figure in sight!

When buying items, do not worry about their intended use. Many puzzles that are designed to test complex problem-solving skills (and are very challenging on that level) may also be used

simply as interesting things to manipulate. Many adult hours of interest and attention can be focused on such things as:
- Rubik's Cube
- Hourglass
- Eight-ball fortune teller
- Sliding numbers puzzle
- Brain teasers
- Magnetic cutouts.

These are just a few suggestions. You and the people you support will probably have many other ideas once given the opportunity to experience a variety of media.

The trick is: Do not take something away; replace it with something appropriate to the person's age. Give options!

4

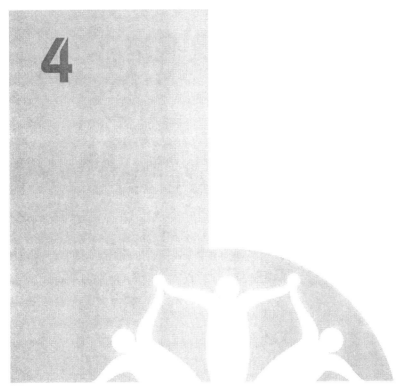

Venturing Beyond the Iron Gate

10

Beyond Mere Integration to Full Inclusion

We have strolled through a brief history of the ways human service workers, family and friends have tried to provide support, care and opportunities to people whose life conditions have cast them as Outsiders. In Section 1, we analyzed the Medical/Custodial Model with its "do for" approach, concerned mostly with providing a safe, isolated, sterile environment for people viewed as being medically defective.

In Section 2, we reviewed the advent of the Developmental Model as a better way of helping people with developmental disabilities progress through the steps of normal child development. We also followed the evolution of the Habilitation Model, noting that this approach was motivated, in part, by the regulations of the Intermediate Care Facility-Mental Retardation program. With its annual plans, the federal program was designed to help people acquire the skills they were thought to need before moving to a less restrictive environment.

In Section 4, we define Universal Enhancement as the vision of a possible future, a paradigm shift that affects how services are funded, organized and provided. Its strategies go to the heart of how people live their lives. Where implemented, these principles are already changing many lives.

A Paradigm Shift

In the preceding sections, much of the groundwork was laid for the paradigm shift of Universal Enhancement. It was necessary to examine the language we use, the definitions that influence our perception of disabilities and handicaps, our understanding of the role of helpers, the use of time, where work should take place, and the values that inform the decisions we make. All of these elements are affected by a paradigm shift. Since Universal Enhancement is such a shift, it alters both our awareness of ourselves and our approach to those who have been cast as Outsiders.

Remember: the guiding principle, the essence of the notion of Universal Enhancement, is inclusion.

The goal is not merely "to rearrange the chairs on the deck of the Titanic," but to urge the building of a new ship. Universal Enhancement is the vehicle that provides the systems and tools required for building that new ship, for the realization of the glorious future desired for and by persons who have been treated as Outsiders.

These tools are uncomplicated and easy to apply. Most importantly, they need not be purchased because they are free. Their use will not violate the current regulations and standards under which we operate. Implementing the tools does not require anyone's permission. They are culture-free and location-free. Since Universal Enhancement is the means we use to get and maintain a life for ourselves, implementation of its strategies will come naturally for many.

Universal Enhancement

What does this mysterious term Universal Enhancement mean? First, let us consider each word. *Universal* means all-embracing, all-reaching, "not limited or restricted." *Enhancement* is defined as "to raise, make greater, improve in quality or condition."[1] Therefore, Universal Enhancement is an increase in the quality of life of all people, without restrictions or limits, regardless of ability or disability.

That seems like a tall order, and so it is. Paradigm shifts always deliver tall orders; they demand stretching our perceptions. Nothing less than this will bring us the world in which all persons are treated as equals, free from institutional oppression. Moving with the flow of

[1] *Webster's New World Dictionary* (New York: Prentice Hall / Macmillan, 1994), 451.

Universal Enhancement will require nothing less than a conversion experience–an epiphany–in people who are invested in the old ways of acting and speaking. Though the changes will be painful for some, I have great hope that they are possible.

Those of us who have lived with the old, dehumanizing way of treating people are the most excited about doing things differently. We should be unabashed in our celebration of this new paradigm and unashamed to proselytize.

Realistically, it will take a great deal of effort and zeal to promote the concepts of Universal Enhancement to "nonbelievers," but the results achieved will only serve to enhance significantly the lives of those we support. In fact, this way of being with the people we support can help resolve many of the problems that have resulted from imposing various other theoretical models on persons who receive services and supports.

In the same manner that elements of religious belief are proven through their "fruits," the tools of Universal Enhancement show themselves potent and true because they bear fruit in the form of better lives for all people. The impact can be seen daily in the lives of many people–those we have the good fortune to serve and those with whom it is our pleasure to work and share support.

A Model of Inclusion

Although Universal Enhancement transcends all models, one model in current use closely resembles its vision. Called Inclusion, this model has gained some currency in the human service field as a result of court orders and empowerment movements that have served to dismantle the old institutional models. Three steps form the cornerstones of the model. They are *integration*, *participation* and *relationships*.

Integration

We usually think of segregation as an injustice perpetrated against persons who are in a minority and who are excluded from the opportunities afforded those in the majority. Segregation means separation–people living in separate worlds, with separate standards and separate goals. It means living on the reservation, in the ghetto or in the institution.

In American history, we are most familiar with the word segregation as it applied to the separation of people on the basis of race. As a nation, we challenged the acceptability of such separation in the historic *Brown v. Board of Education of Topeka, Kansas*, ruling by the Supreme Court in 1954. In that decision, taking the position that separate is inherently unequal, Chief Justice Earl Warren wrote:

> To separate [Negro children] from others of similar age and qualifications solely because of their race generates a feeling of inferiority as to their status in the community that may affect their hearts and minds in a way unlikely ever to be undone.... We conclude that in the field of public education the doctrine of "separate but equal" has no place. Separate educational facilities are inherently unequal.[2]

It was twenty years before the same principle was applied to children who had disabilities (PL 94-142, The Right to Education of All Handicapped Children Act of 1975), and even today, mainstreaming is not as common in public schools as it ought to be. Children with disabilities are still educated in separate, self-contained classrooms, often in separate, special schools. Indeed, *special* is often a code word for *separate*, as in Special Olympics or Special Education.

However, segregation does more than diminish opportunities for Outsiders who are victims of segregation. Segregation of people into separate groups denies the majority the opportunity to know people in other groups. This "not knowing" (the literal meaning of ignorance) creates prejudice, a judgment that occurs prior to knowing.

And prejudice allows people to be judged on the basis of what we think we know about them (judging the contents by the label), rather than on our relationships with real, individual people. I had a friend who grew up in a suburb of Chicago, which, as late as 1965, had all

---

[2] Brown v. Board of Education of Topeka, Kansas, 74 Sup. Ct. 686 (1954)

> **Integration**
>
> **Integration:** (noun) 1. The act of process or an instance of integrating; as incorporation as equals into society or an organization of individuals of different groups (as races)

white residents. (Chicago has, for many decades, been home to the largest contiguous, African American population in the country.) The high school of twenty-five hundred students was all white. The Boy Scout troop was all white. The church was all white. Though no laws barred people of other racial and ethnic groups from living there, the suburb had maintained its "whiteness." It practiced *de facto* segregation.

How many relationships do you think my friend had with African-Americans or persons of Hispanic or Asian background? Of course, none. Sadly, in communities where persons with dark skin, persons of Buddhist faith, or persons with disabilities live only with "their own kind," no one has a chance to learn from the other. When my friend started college in New York and lived with a Jewish roommate, just think of what he learned from his roommate's family and they from him.

One of the first characteristics of an institution (described in Section 1) is that it keeps people remote from the mainstream of society, isolated from opportunities for learning and relationships. People with disabilities were once believed to have an entirely different set of needs from those of us who lived in homes and apartments in the cities and towns of this country. In order to meet their special needs (carefully avoiding any reference to society's need not to have to see and interact with them), persons with disabilities were put into facilities designed to care for them. They were placed there. The same thing was done with Native Americans under the guise of protecting them. Our elders, too, are often placed in nursing homes, supposedly for their own good.

MAXIM: *Being a priority on a placement list is not seeing the light at the end of the tunnel. It is standing on the edge of a precipice.*

Such placement usually deprives everyone concerned of opportunities. The policy of segregation on the basis of difference (competence, skin color or cultural background) also deprives the persons who remain behind. Normatives, the people who live in communities sanitized of anyone who is too different from the norm, are denied the opportunity of knowing and interacting with individuals who possess charm, humor and their own quirky wisdom.

Robert Perske, in his wonderful 1980 book *New Life in the Neighborhood*, wrote about the advent of community placements such as group homes: "Neighborhoods will discover that there are not enough of these citizens with handicaps to go around. Some neighborhoods will have to go without!"[3]

Participation

Integration of people typically treated as Outsiders is an exciting and necessary first step. When group homes first began opening in towns and neighborhoods, welcoming people from large, centralized facilities, many believed they had it made at last.

There was excitement about people who were deinstitutionalized. They could now attend a neighborhood church, rather than just going to the chapel on the institution campus. They also had the opportunity

---

[3] Robert and Martha Perske, *New Life in the Neighborhood* (Nashville, TN: Abingdon Press, 1980) 30.

to go to a movie or the grocery store in the community. Integration had been achieved, and many believed that was what it was all about. But we were shortsighted, limited by a vision that did not encompass the dreams and desires of the people we sought to serve.

Fortunately, Universal Enhancement's new paradigm shift forces one to ask deeper, more complex questions. The more relevant question is, "What are they doing in the integrated setting?" Yes, there were men and women going to the neighborhood movie theater, but our excitement blinded us to what was often happening. Staff were taking them.

Well, what is wrong with that?

Keep 'Em Dependent

Limiting opportunity, options, education and experience helps assure dependence.

Oppressor	**Oppressed**
Chauvinistic husband	Abused wife
White slave owner	Black slave
Loan shark	Debtor
Drug pusher	Drug addict
Pimp	Prostitute
Coal baron	Coal miner
	Person with intellectual or developmental disability

The oppressor has always known this about the oppressed.

The problem is that integration, in and of itself, does little to improve the quality of a person's life. Often, it fails to address many kinds of challenging behavior that are learned in institutional settings. And, alone it cannot help a person grow, develop and become more independent; it lacks an essential element of a quality life.

Participation: Affecting Your Environment

To measure the degree of participation in an activity, we must ask, "In what ways is that person involved in the activity?" Several issues arise around participation in a trip to the movie theater. Will the man or

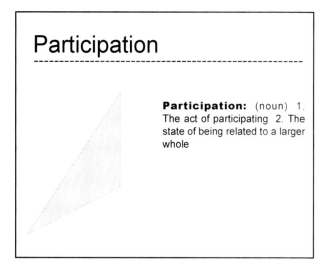

woman going to the movies be allowed to carry the money and buy the movie ticket, or will the staff carry the money and buy the ticket? Who will choose which movie to go to? Who will hand the ticket to the ticket taker? Who will keep the ticket stub? Who will decide where to sit? Who has the option to decide whether the movie is good or not? Who will decide when it is time to leave? Unless the answer is the

person who is receiving support, integration has brought no significant improvement over institutional life.

If you feel that this describes a very unrealistic expectation for a person with disabilities, you may respond with questions of your own: "Won't some people always have to be taken to the movies?" If the person is so physically limited that his arms are contracted and they can hardly move, or he cannot see or speak, how can he buy a ticket or choose a movie?

The answer (described fully in Chapter 6) is: We are going to take what we can get closest to what we (they) want. A person may need almost total assistance, but as I offer the assistance needed, I am going to think aloud, "Now, Bryan, we're going to get the ticket. We need that five dollars you placed in your billfold before we left." And, even if he attempts to put the money in his mouth, that is not a justification for denying Bryan the opportunity to remove the bills from his wallet, even though he may require a lot of support in doing so.

The person's limitation is not a sanction for us to *do for* but a mandate to assist. As Bryan's assistant, I become his agent, working on his behalf, remaining silent and in the background until summoned by the occasion of his need for me. As a support staff, we must be quiet

Being Missed

Where is Susan? Have you seen her today?

Having relationships - and being part of your community means being missed by others when absent.

voices in the background. We must remain transparent, for it is that person's life.

Continuing with the example of the trip to the movie theater, Bryan may need me to assist him in getting his money out of his pocket or wallet and presenting it at the ticket window. If Bryan is unable to reach the window, I may have to assist him further, but as his agent, I will still ask, "Which movie do you want to see, *Space Bimbos* or *Godzilla Goes Hawaiian?*"

If he makes no apparent response, but I know Bryan likes loud monster films, I say, "Oh, *Godzilla*. Okay, one ticket for *Godzilla*." I may have to assist in getting the ticket from the window by placing it in Bryan's hand, on his lap or in his pocket. And, I will continue my running commentary: "Bryan, here's your ticket. You'll need to give it to the ticket taker when we get inside the door."

Next, I may have to assist Bryan by pushing his wheelchair through the door. If so, I will continue commenting aloud: "These doors are hard to open when you use a wheelchair."

All the while, Bryan may appear unresponsive to anything in his environment, but he is actually doing quite a lot. He is listening to me as I think out loud, and his acceptance of my extensive assistance may be, at this time, the fullest extent to which he can participate.

Seeing the Individual

Can you identify these traits in the persons for whom you provide support?

Compassion	Gregarious	Honest	Independent
Integrity	Fidelity	Kind	Optimistic
Sincere	Industrious	Sensitive	Cautious
Assertive	Forgiving	Shy	Patient
Empathetic	Determined	Spontaneous	Principled
Creative	Motivated	Generous	

We must be able to see through the individual's disabilities and challenges and appreciate the beauty of their personality.

The important point is that I am *doing with* Bryan rather than *doing for* him.

The major difference between doing for and doing with is in our mindset, our way of thinking about what we are doing. It is an attitude, if you will. In using the tools of Universal Enhancement, I must think of myself as going to the movies with Bryan rather than taking him to the movies. It is this approach that makes all the difference.

If I adopt the *do with* mindset, I must acknowledge and respect the fact that it is Bryan's money, Bryan's ticket, Bryan's refreshments and Bryan's place to sit. When I arrive at this realization, I am prepared to act as the support and assistant that I need to be. I will know my place and my function; I am to give Bryan the support he needs in order to enjoy his Saturday afternoon at the movies. This is participation—when a person is assisted in doing what he or she wants to do, not toted around like a doll or a pet, nor towed like a boat.

There is an edifying scene in the movie, *Scent of a Woman*. A young student, hired to assist a retired colonel who is blind, takes hold of the colonel's arm to try to lead him through the doors at the airport. The colonel snaps at the student, "Are you blind?!"

The student, dumbfounded, does not know what to say.

The colonel barks again, "I said, 'Are you blind?'"

The student answers sheepishly, "No."

"Then don't grab my arm," replies the Colonel. "I grab your arm."[4]

It seems almost petty, but the difference is crucial. Applying the principles of Universal Enhancement to facilitate participation guarantees that the one receiving assistance is in charge. And being in charge—making decisions and choices about one's life—is what gives that life meaning and dignity. If the assistant is in charge, the person who needs help is just an appendage, an object to be scheduled, taken, fed, moved and programmed.

If integration fails to lead to participation, the doors to a quality life remain closed. Let us not, through default, create little institutions on

---

[4] *Scent of a Woman*, prod. and dir. Martin Brest (Universal City, CA: MCA / Universal Home Video, 1993) videocassette.

Introduction...
Making Community Connections

"Joe, I'd like for you to meet John."

every block, in which people with differences live out their lives unrelated to the Normatives who live around them and are consequently precluded from enriching the lives of their neighbors and neighborhoods.

It is also only through participation in life's activities that relationships can be developed. If we take Linda to the grocery store, clamp her hand firmly to the shopping cart and direct her through the aisles as we do her shopping for her, what is gained? How is Linda's life enhanced? This is little better than sitting in the day room watching staff-selected soap operas.

Only through interaction with the other shoppers, the produce manager, the checkout clerks and the baggers, does the shopping trip take on real value and meaning.

MAXIM: *Getting* out *(of the institution) is easy; getting* in *(to the community) is hard.*

Does this sound familiar? Remember "interacting with media?" When a level of meaningful participation is realized, the whole community serves as the media for learning and growing. We could have a whole training program that consists of nothing but spending the day walking around town, meeting new people, encountering novel

situations and meeting whatever challenges might present themselves—in short, participating in the town's, city's or neighborhood's ongoing life. You see, getting out of the institution is the easy part. Getting into the community is much, much harder—for the community must be built.

TALE
Helen and the Bell Choir

I once met a woman named Helen who lived in a large metropolitan area on the East Coast. She was only three feet long, lying down. And lying down was where she was all the time. Her body was so contracted that she spent her day supported by a padded, plywood board, maintained in position with Velcro straps. Due to a condition diagnosed as similar to anencephaly ("no brain"), she lacked vision and hearing.

She was forty-four years old, qualified to be considered an adult. But, the staff at the institution where she lived had given her a baby rattle so that she would "have something to do."

Helen moved out of the institution into a "home" with several other women. Despite her apparent disabilities, the staff in the home bonded with her. One of the staff (we'll call her Sue) got the novel idea of going to church with Helen.

As Helen didn't do much, she did not make many demands on the people who were with her. She didn't make any noises or engage in any behavior that would cause a disturbance. So Helen and Sue attended church together uneventfully.

A number of people who had very limited physical and cognitive abilities lived in Helen's home. Extensive occupational therapy services were provided to all of them, including Helen. The occupational therapist directed the staff to assist Helen in the use of a rolling pin. So staff would roll it back and forth to increase Helen's range of motion and palmar grasp–a functional outcome.

But rolling a rolling pin back and forth when there's no dough to be rolled is not a meaningful activity. It is an activity completely lacking in one essential element that is required to turn engagement into a valued learning opportunity. So Sue tried to think of a more meaningful way for Helen to work toward increasing her range of motion and improving her palmar grasp.

As Sue searched for options, she thought about the church they attended. It had a wonderful bell choir to which Helen responded. Sue could see by her facial expression that she could sense the vibration of the bells when they were played. One day, Sue approached the director of the bell choir and asked if it would be possible for Helen to participate. The director must have thought Sue was joking. This staff person wanted a helpless woman who was supported by a padded, plywood board and had no vision, hearing or palmar grasp to play in the choir!

The director finally agreed that Helen could attend some rehearsals. She would be attached to the cart that provided her mobility, and Sue would be sitting next to her. In order to simplify the task for Helen, Sue asked the director if she could play one of the lower tone bells, one that was not played as often as the others. Sue offered

assistance and support by placing the bell in Helen's hand and moving her hand when it was Helen's time to ring the bell.

Each ringer in a bell choir is required to sit in the same place each time so that the bells are always in the same order. An older woman named Betty occupied the position next to Helen. At first, Betty felt a little uneasy about the situation. She was anxious about having to sit next to a little woman strapped to a padded, plywood board. Helen was certainly not the kind of person with whom one usually develops a social relationship.

But, as Sue persisted in being very friendly on Helen's behalf, Betty gradually overcame her discomfort in Helen's presence. Sue and Betty began talking on Sundays, though Betty never talked directly to Helen. Then one Sunday, as Sue was assisting Helen to ring her bell, Helen let out a laugh. This was very unusual for Helen, for no one had ever heard her make any kind of sound.

Betty, sitting next to Helen as always, was struck by the humor and, without thinking, said, "Helen, did something tickle you?"

"Isn't that wonderful?" Sue responded on Helen's behalf. "Helen just laughed."

That broke the ice. The next Sunday when Helen came into the choir loft, Betty said, "Good morning, Helen. How are you doing this morning? Your dress really looks lovely. It's a nice day outside today, isn't it?" Betty had begun making casual conversation, just as all of us do when we're starting to get to know someone.

The chats continued for a few more Sundays. Betty began to develop a rapport with Helen. Betty is one of those people who understand intuitively what it means to think out loud and take what you can get closest to what you (they) want. She is a person who has water in her well.

One Saturday afternoon a few weeks later, Betty called the group home and asked for Sue. Betty was a little hesitant at first, beating around the bush as though there was something she wanted to say but didn't quite know how. Finally, she blurted out, "I don't know if this would be appropriate or not. I mean, I know you must have rules and things at that home. But I was wondering...do you think that tomorrow, after church, you and Helen could come over to my house for dinner?"

A connection had been made. A relationship had been formed. And that is what life is all about. That is inclusion.

VALUED RELATIONSHIPS

How many relationships do the people you support have other than with:

- Family members
- Paid relationships such as support staff, physician, dentist
- Individuals with disabilities with whom they work or live

What is the relationship between an individual's competence and the number of valued relationships they have beyond those stated above?

What supports do you need to offer that will facilitate cognitively and physically challenged people in forming valued relationships?

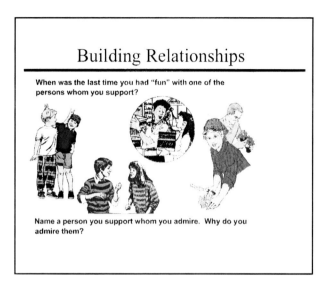

Relationship

Inclusion is achieved through the social interactions that arise from participation in life's activities. Every relationship that you and I have entered into (excluding relationships with family members) has occurred because of our participation—our participation as an employee, student, volunteer, or member of bowling leagues or hobby groups. Participation in life's activities is the source of relationships.

Participation is the key that unlocks the opportunity for people to form and develop meaningful relationships. And meaningful relationships are the most important elements of almost everyone's vision of quality of life. Relationships are what inclusion is all about. In fact, "relationships" could be a one-word definition of inclusion.

If you provide support for, are related to, or know of, a person who has been segregated as an Outsider (as the result of any characteristic viewed as socially unacceptable), ask yourself how many relationships that person has with people who are not immediate family members. How many of the relationships involve a person who is not paid to provide support services? How many involve someone who is not a member of the same Outsiders group?

The answer, too often, is zero. In those instances where a person has four or five relationships, it is likely that the person in question demonstrates considerable competence (is able to slip past the Gatekeepers). This should not surprise us. How are people supposed to develop meaningful, life-enhancing relationships if they only have opportunities to spend time with family, support workers and others of their kind? How much meaning would your life have if your valued relationships were few or restricted?

TOOLBOX
Taking Stock

Here is a good way to assess the quality of relationships in a group with which you work.

1. Ask everyone to think of one person he or she knows who has been excluded because of some personal characteristic.

2. Ask: How many relationships does that person have with people who are not paid to support him/her, are not members of his/her family, and are not also excluded due to the same life circumstance? Have group members show the number of relationships by raising their hands with fingers extended. A closed fist equals zero relationships, one finger is one, two fingers is two, and so on.

3. Have participants look all around the room at the raised hands. Ask them to take stock of the closed fists versus the hands with fingers. It is always a chilling experience to see the forest of raised fists.

4. Ask the group to think about the cases where several fingers are raised. You can almost guarantee that the person represented by raised fingers has more competence than the person represented by a fist. The more challenging the person's disability, the fewer relationships that person is likely to experience.

Relationships are the key to the enrichment of people's lives, not just of people with Outsider status, but of all people. In order to achieve a high quality of life, all three elements of our quality of life triangle must be present–integration, participation and relationship. When all elements are built upon, the person who is newly returned to our communities from exile in the land of Outsiders will be able to establish a presence, and finally have a life and be somebody.

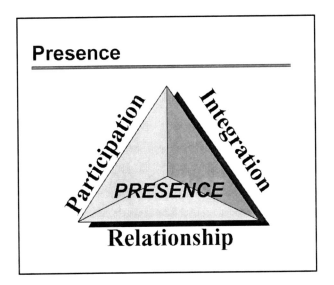

The Elements of Getting a Life

Some of the tools used to facilitate and support inclusion for all people were discussed in preceding chapters. Techniques of inclusion such as "Take what you can get closest to what you (they) want," and "Don't do anything alone," are part of the process of helping people grow, develop and become more independent. As people become more integrated into the mainstream of their communities, they have more opportunities to participate in the ongoing activities of community life. Participation then leads to relationships, which foster inclusion.

Anyone who has used the "training" techniques of the Habilitative Model years must sense immediately that such techniques as backward chaining and strict command structures are very different from the *do with* activities proposed. Training techniques of the old type are part of the *do to* mentality, the old paradigm. They are remnants of the habilitation principle, stating that people need to learn new skills in order to move into a less restrictive environment (one with an increased range of options). But, as mentioned earlier, we need to advocate that everybody is ready for everything, right now.

Going beyond mere training to encompass the concept of support generates an almost limitless set of opportunities and possibilities. We do not have to wait until people learn to be more independent if we are willing to support and encourage full inclusion in all activities of society and community. Indeed, interdependence–relying on a network of friends, coworkers and neighbors for assistance as needed–is the way most of us Normatives live our lives. Why should it be any different for a person whose needs for support are of a different type or more extensive than our own?

Clearly, it is no different. That is the central judgment and precept of Universal Enhancement. The outcome is the same whether this judgment is based on some variation of the Golden Rule (Do unto others as you would have them do unto you); some theological belief that all human beings are children of God; or some pragmatic and introspective understanding that our lives are enriched by being open to relationships with all kinds of people. No person is completely alien to us, so different that his or her needs and desires are incomprehensible and strange to us.

MAXIM: *Getting* a life for people, and coaching them into it...is the intervention. ™

When we accept the challenge to tear down the barriers that separate us from other people, we immediately know what to do when advocating for Outsiders, because we know what *we* need in order to live complete, satisfied lives. You do not need university degrees or clinical experience to begin the process of Universal Enhancement. All you need is an open mind and a willing heart. If we enthusiastically support people in realizing the possibilities and potentials of their lives, it should be easy to find ways to become valued co-contributors in all the relationships we form with people who have been seen as Outsiders. The tools that follow are merely guidelines, pointing in the directions where we need to aim our efforts as we all work together to achieve Universal Enhancement.

Supporting Inclusionary Behavior

Inclusion does not happen overnight with the waving of advocacy's magic wand. The road to inclusion is often a long one with hills to climb and sharp bends to negotiate. The vision of Universal Enhancement would be nothing but a map of fantasyland if it did not offer a vehicle for helping people move from Outsider status to inclusion. The tools of Universal Enhancement will help you help others get past the Gatekeepers and other obstacles that barricade the road.

The process of providing supports (the process of Universal Enhancement) is not amorphous. It is a logical structure that provides opportunities to participate in the natural flow of life, in basic routines that are often referred to as *positive rituals*. As a person moves from a place where he was not valued or provided the opportunity to participate in life's positive rituals, he faces an acclimation process. One does not move instantly into a life of enrichment.

The way we relate to that person as we support inclusion is multi-layered. We must employ a variety of supports as we teach him how to shed his Outsider status and overcome obstacles to a valued life. But, it can be difficult to know where to start. Part of our role in the transition process is to lead the person down a path where opportunities to experience the artifacts of life can be found.

On this path, we operate under a *do with* model, serving as collaborators who help people realize their hopes, dreams and desires. Those of us who are paid for this work really do "work for clients" when we see ourselves in this way; we are engaged to act in their behalf. This way of working truly puts the support recipient in the driver's seat. *He* makes choices, sets goals and determines priorities.

The following processes can serve as stepping stones that help us support a person who has been negatively affected by institutional characteristics.

- Mend
- Socialize
- Connect
- Communicate
- Initiate.

Mend

The first step, *mending*, is necessary because many people come to us with something broken. Long years of institutional living may have broken their spirits or wills. Their choice-making ability may be rusty with disuse. And, most importantly, the ties that bind people with one another in a community have been severed. A time of mending is needed.

This mending process used to be called *stabilization*, a term inherited from the Medical/Custodial Model, wherein the "patient" who cannot be cured can at least be "stabilized." Stabilization was viewed as the best outcome possible for a person who was not deemed capable of having a regular life. The Medical/Custodial Model used admission as treatment. Once you were in the safe facility, your condition could be stabilized. Does that sound like a goal you or your loved ones have for your lives? Do you want your life to be stable? Probably not. You probably want variety, change, adventure and challenge in your life.

Design Universal Life Stiles
The former Outsider who is trying to be reintegrated into the ongoing life of his community faces formidable obstacles. Gatekeepers of various stripes, from fearful neighbors to skeptical employers, do their best to keep the barriers intact between the world of the Outsider and the protected world of Us. As we assist former Outsiders to get a life, several different approaches could be taken to tear down these barriers.

MEND

- **Design Life Stiles.**
  - Identify the obstacles in that person's life.
  - Modify the environment.

- **Redirect and Protect.**
  - Offer gentle physical support.
  - Support choice making.

- **Consider a temporary medication plan.**
  - Assess and review the need for medication.
  - Start low, go slow.

The protests and rights legislation of the radical advocate could be adopted in an attempt to smash the barriers. But, that approach is liable to bring a backlash that would seriously limit the universal (for all people) element of what we are trying to accomplish. Or, we could teach Outsiders patience, asking them to understand that many people are ignorant and scared, and that they (the Outsiders) must wait apologetically until some Gatekeeper becomes enlightened enough to crack the gate enough for admission.

Still another approach is to face the barrier head-on and find a way over it. In rural areas, pastures are sometimes delimited with fences made of rock and stone. Instead of using gates (difficult to build into a rock wall), people use stiles, steps built over the wall that allow people to walk easily up and over the barrier. Life Stiles are not specifically designed for certain groups of individuals but apply to all people. A common bond we share is that barriers of one type or another challenge each of us. What makes us unique and individual is the approach we take to overcoming those barriers. When used as the means for overcoming obstacles in a person's life, these steps are called Life Stiles.

The first activity in building Life Stiles is the identification of barriers. What are the obstacles to this particular person's inclusion? That is, are we trying to step over a two-foot high wall of loose rocks that may require only a steadying hand to surmount? Or, is it a five-foot wall that calls for building several sturdy steps? Or, perhaps we are trying to scale a ten-foot wall of finished stone that will require ropes, climbing gear and a couple of pulleys.

It is important to note that identifying barriers in a person's life is very different from identifying that person's deficits (as we did under the Developmental and Habilitation models). Blaming a person for the wall before her, or the gate slammed in her face, will not help her get to the other side. What will help is the identification of an obstacle as a challenge that can be overcome through creativity and perseverance.

My friend Donald is just beginning a job at Hardee's. He has to complete many tasks, such as wiping tables, washing trays, emptying

trash, filling condiment bottles and cleaning the parking lot. He cannot follow the typical task checklist because he cannot read. Now, we could identify his lack of reading ability as the obstacle and tell him he can have a job as soon as he learns to read. Or, we could design a Life Stile for overcoming the barrier, such as a picture card that helps Donald remember what tasks he needs to complete.

Life Stiles overcome barriers right now. There is no waiting for someone else to change (the myth of the enlightenment of Gatekeepers), or waiting until the Outsider acquires new skills (the myth of habilitation). We identify the obstacle and design some way of getting over it. We come up with ways to modify the environment, rather than to modify the person. To do this, we must go beyond individual strengths and needs assessments that lead to training programs. We develop *assessments of obstacles* that lead to lists of creative Life Stiles. If we get out our hammers and nails and help an Outsider build steps to get over walls, she and we will be walking in the neighboring field in no time.

The ever vigilant, astute reader asks, "But what do you do when confronted by someone who wants to take your head off or throw the TV set through the living room window? What kind of Life Stile do I build for him?"

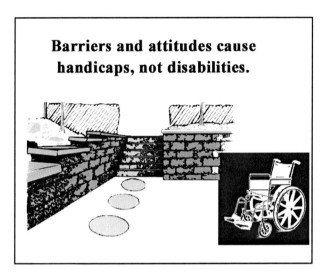

Barriers and attitudes cause handicaps, not disabilities.

Answering this concerned person by suggesting all she has to do is form relationships and encourage community inclusion would be naive. She is dealing with challenging behaviors that have arisen in response to the kinds of life circumstances that thwart the usual processes of socialization. The behaviors do not disintegrate or disappear overnight, nor are they "cured" with this process. The primary purpose of Universal Enhancement is to improve the quality of life. So, introducing a person to a world of Universal Enhancement often results in a secondary purpose of reducing challenging behavior.

A person is not going to get the supports she needs if everyone is afraid of her. She is not going to succeed in even the first step, that of integration, if her behavior is so threatening and damaging that community officials feel justified in locking her away in a nursing home, a juvenile detention center or a state psychiatric hospital.

Often, the first thing we need to do in helping someone mend is to arrange a "prosthetic environment." Such an environment, responsive to the needs of a particular person, immediately provides a situation that will give that person the best chance of beginning the process of mending. For example, we provide the wife who is abused with a shelter where she can heal from her wounds and make a start at getting a new, safe life. Or, we provide the person with alcoholism with a detox opportunity, a place where he is prevented from obtaining alcohol long enough to begin the process of recovery. Notice that these examples are actually a limiting of the person's freedoms and opportunities. Such limitation is acceptable if it is only the first step in the process.

TOOLBOX
The Three I's of Consequation

During a period of mending, we may need to apply specific consequences to behavior that is serving as a barrier to inclusion. To ensure that these consequences are truly opportunities for learning and not punitive reactions, we can follow the Three I's.
Consequences must be:
- *Immediate* - responsive to the current event. Never threaten; never promise.
- *Intense* - stronger than competing events and rewards.
- *Impersonal* - directed at the behavior, not at the person.

The provision of a temporary prosthetic environment is similar to the way we child-proof a house where a two-year-old lives. Rather than fighting an hourly battle to get little Johnny to leave the valuable Ming vase alone, we just put it up in the closet and replace it with a cheaper one from a discount store. When we stop having to replace the inexpensive vase, the Ming will come back to the display shelf. Similarly, in residential settings for people who have challenging behaviors, we adapt the environment to the needs of the individual.

MAXIM: *The least restrictive environment is determined by the person with the most severe disability.*

The process of engineering a supportive environment differs from the process of environmental sterilization that goes on in institutional

> **Environmental Restrictions**
>
> The restrictions and adaptations made to respond to the unique protective oversight needs of each individual serves to restrict the freedom and options of others in the environment.
>
> | Concern | Institutional Restriction |
> |---|---|
> | Leaves without supervision/permission | Install door alarms |
> | Uses mops and broom handles as weapons | Lock up items |
> | Shreds linens | Lock up items |
> | Afflicts self-injury with knives | Lock up items |
> | Flushes toilet papers rolls down toilet | Lock up items |
> | Ingests caustic substances (i.e., cologne, detergent) | Lock up items |
>
> *Seek Creative Alternatives*

settings. The latter results in the least restrictive environment being determined by the person with the most severe disability. That is to say, unfortunately, we modify the environment to address the needs of the person with the most severe disability, regardless of the level of competency of the other persons living there. Creating a supportive environment, by contrast, is more like the procedure for supporting choice making. Also called *individualized adaptation*, the process begins with a small set of options and increases the range of options as the person demonstrates increased choice-making ability.

If a person's level of aggressive behavior is so intense that the changes needed to help her mend would impinge on all others with whom she lives, then she may need to live by herself for a while. The goal is to avoid posing challenges that are too difficult for a person to meet, or obstacles that set her up for failure. When the challenges are mediated by good environmental engineering (a form of Life Stile), the person is likely to be more successful in dealing with opportunities for successful inclusion.

An important principle here, when making environmental adaptations in the name of mending, is that we do not want to make any changes that remove the possibility of learning to adapt. We do not want to remove opportunities in the process of providing supports. This is a tricky and difficult challenge.

An elegant example of "a difference that doesn't make a difference" is the installation of curtains that are attached to their sliding hooks by means of plastic snaps. If someone, in a property-destroying rage, pulls the curtains down, they can be easily reattached. This is a much more creative response than the typical institutional reaction of removing curtains entirely. By coming up with a creative solution to the problem of curtain ripping, we are developing a true prosthetic environment, not just a sterilized one. The challenge is to make sure a person has all the media he or she needs for developing a meaningful quality of life while at the same time taking steps to assure everyone's safety.

Redirect and Protect

Sometimes, a person needs to be stopped from harming herself or others. We cannot stand by and watch someone bite pieces out of her arm or stand in the middle of a busy street. If we cannot talk a person into directing her energy and attention into a more appropriate behavior, we may have to lay hands on her and offer gentle restraint.

However, when we find ourselves using restraint, it is important to understand that it is a form of support, no different in function from a wheelchair or a job coach. Stopping a person from hitting other people, using as little force as possible along with an attitude of respect and concern, allows him to do something he is unable to do on his own–stop hurting himself or others.

Within the value orientation of Universal Enhancement, restraint is not used as punishment, therapy or training. It is not an exercise in controlling power. Rather, restraint is applied out of *empathy*, out of a desire to assure that the person does not hurt himself or others. It is a support that is offered only so much as it is needed because the blocked behavior would otherwise interfere with that person's ability to realize his or her own dreams and goals. If life has no meaning, people will behave in a way to cause the lives of others to have no value or meaning.

Restraint is something *done with* someone, while encouraging him to do as much as he can on his own. It is never something *done to* someone, out of a sense that we have a right to control a person whom we see as less worthy or less powerful than ourselves.

One way to keep this distinction in mind is to remember the principle of *redirection*: never try to get a person to stop doing something; get him to do something else. Restraint is not a closed box of tight control. It is, rather, a way of directing a person toward an acceptable way of dealing with rage, frustration or fear. We must always leave one side of the "corral" open. That side must face in the direction that takes a person toward success.

Redirection is similar to the approach used in some gentle martial arts practices. The energy of attack and destruction is deflected in an alternative direction. Redirection leads the person to an increased ability to behave in ways that will increase his chances of acceptance and full inclusion.

It may seem strange, in a discussion of restraint and redirection, to bring up the topic of choice making again. However, having the ability to choose from among desirable options is a key element in getting a life. Every person wants to have some control over his or her

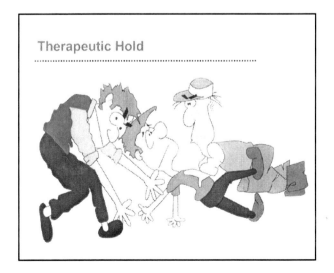

Therapeutic Hold

own life. And, in the presence of institutional characteristics, personal control is often taken away from the Outsider who, staff conclude, is unable to control himself. This sets into motion a vicious, descending cycle. The lack of opportunity for choice making leads the person to try to control his environment through troubling and challenging means. Staff then impose more external control, and the situation just gets worse.

> **MAXIM:** *The intervention for many inappropriate behaviors is not seclusion, but inclusion.* ™

Instead of engaging in this counterproductive control cycle, it is best to offer meaningful, measured options as alternatives to violence and disruption. The three-sided corral model says, "Over here. This is where you can be successful. Which of these alternatives would you like to try?" When people see a light at the end of the tunnel, they very often cease struggling to get off the track.

It is crucial that we keep this vision in mind as we use prosthetic environments and the presentation of options as Life Stiles for overcoming of obstacles.

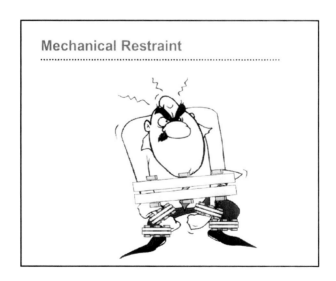

Mechanical Restraint

Medication: Start Low, Go Slow

Psychotropic medication should be seen in the same light as restraint. It is a support that may be needed by a person to help her grow and develop. It should never serve as an expedient solution that relieves us of the responsibility of supplying enough supports, staff assistance, environmental modification or opportunity to make choices.

MAXIM: *Start low, go slow.*

Medication should serve, whenever possible, as a temporary intervention. Like the crutch or cane used only until a broken leg heals, it is not an essential part of "treatment." It should never be used to remove any meaningful control a person has over his life. Of course, there will be persons who do not heal past their need for medication, despite our best efforts at helping them get a life. For these persons, medication is more like a prosthetic limb used by a person whose leg was amputated. It would be unreasonable to expect him to do without it. Even for a person who demonstrates a continued need for psychopharmaceutical support, we must always strive to help him use only as much support as is truly necessary for his particular circumstance. This requires that

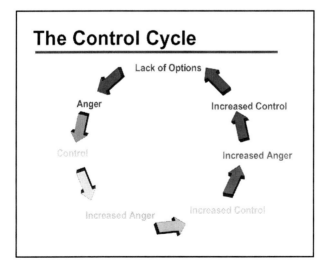

medication be used only with clear documentation of its effectiveness, and at the lowest possible, effective dose.

Mending is only the first step in supporting inclusion. Mending activities are most often necessary when people are trying to make the transition from institutional-type settings to environments with minimal external controls. Mending sometimes becomes necessary because a former Outsider's reputation has been tarnished, and the staff or other people in his life are afraid. If everyone around a person fears him, he will not have much opportunity to get on with his life.

Mending is often the most difficult and challenging task of inclusion. But, when approached with an attitude of respect and support, it can be the step that brings the most immediate benefit to the person who has lived for years under the burdens of institutional systems.

Socialize

Another process often made necessary by having lived under the burden of institutional characteristics is *socialization*. Many people, finding themselves in an environment over which they have little control or where they are treated with disrespect or abuse, will develop a self-protective style of relating to a world they see as hazardous. It is not unusual to hear staff who provide supports for such a person say, "He likes to be by himself," or "I can't get her to do things with the others." These caring staff people are confronted with the challenge of helping someone come out of a shell that has served him well, perhaps for most of his life.

Develop Tolerance of Others

The first step in socialization uses the maxim we explored in Chapter 6: "Take what you can get closest to what you want." (from Lee Graber) It also follows the *classical conditioning* paradigm for developing a person's tolerance for social interaction. We let the person with the defensive style know that she is in control of the level of interaction, but we keep assisting her in getting a little closer to the desired outcome (social interaction) with each engagement.

> ## SOCIALIZE
>
> - Develop Tolerance of others.
>   - Teach kindness.
>   - Interact with others in non-task focused ways.
>   - Allow people to adjust to their own personal space.
>
> - Promote "Unconditional Positive Regard."
>   - Provide attention and praise for each person's interests and gifts.
>   - Facilitate occasions for successful interaction.
>
> - Introduce giving and receiving.
>   - Encourage people to give and do for others.
>   - Promote expressions of appreciation.

We do this with the conviction that wanting to be by herself is in the same class as wanting her Little Mermaid coloring book. It is a lifestyle based on incomplete information and experience. We firmly believe that when someone learns the joys of social interaction and the opportunities that come with relationships, she will likely choose to be social, at least to some degree. Our task is to introduce the defensive person gradually to the joys of inclusion.

Rejection of social relationships is often the result of an institutional emphasis on tasks, or a life where the *relationship experience* is punitive and/or painful. When the staff/resident ratio is low and supported routines are lacking, the interactions that do occur happen as they fit into staff schedules or involve tasks to be completed. As a result, the person may associate interaction with someone trying to get her to do something, or superficial give and take. We can help someone develop a tolerance for others by relating to her in other than task-focused ways.

Promote Positive, Unconditional Regard

One way to diminish task focus is to act in ways that fly in the face of the *do to* style of training that uses all desired items and events as reinforcers, things received contingent on the presence of a particular target behavior. Socialization is one area in which the strict management of contingencies may be inappropriate. When we are helping a person who has been deprived of life experiences to mend, we must emphasize unconditional positive regard for that person. People in Groups I (the Revered) and II (Us), [see Chapter 1] often exhibit such regard, despite a person's challenging behavior.

We call this courtesy or kindness. Expressions of kindness are the primary lubricant that keeps the wheels of community relationships rolling. Kindness should be modeled for people who may have little experience receiving it. And, we must offer them opportunities to demonstrate attitudes of kindness.

Introduce Giving and Receiving

People with intellectual and other disabilities have been on the receiving end of giving far too long. They are commonly seen as needy and dependent, with nothing to give in return. Imagine how that would make you feel. Giving to others can be essential to building your self-esteem, your capacity for kindness and caring, and *relationships*.

An excellent way of learning kindness is to volunteer to perform a caring act. Volunteering can also be an entree into community participation. A good example is when a person requiring pervasive supports volunteers once a week at the local Humane Society shelter. Doing some simple task for the animals gives him an opportunity to be successful in giving. And, for some of us, it is a lot easier to show kindness toward orphaned animals than toward impatient store managers.

> **MAXIM:** *Being an adult is a bilateral process; one must know how to give as well as receive.* ™

Even if a person can do nothing more than hold the kittens for a few minutes, this simple act encompasses integration, participation and relationships. For instance, a person who successfully helps out on this level may meet someone (another volunteer) who will issue an invitation to join in the next Humane Society walk-a-thon.

Participating in the walk-a-thon earns the walker (or wheeler) a T-shirt, which proclaims, "I am somebody. I have something to give."

Often, a person who has been labeled an Outsider does not receive appreciation because she does not know how to offer it. Our task becomes that of showing her how to say thank you, write a note of appreciation, or give a gift in return for a favor. Expressing appreciation to others makes you a more attractive person. It is an important element of socialization.

Socialization means becoming socially and emotionally acclimated to a new environment. It could almost be called *decompression*

TOOLBOX

An Operant Definition of Bonding

May occur at one, or all of three levels, and may be reciprocal.

- Level One: One person becomes a signal for the availability of reinforcement of another (Discriminative Stimulus Function).
- Level Two: One person becomes a reinforcer for another in regard to specific situations/context and specific behavior (Acquired Reinforcer Value).
- Level Three: One person becomes a reinforcer for another in a generalized fashion across situations, and in regard to a variety of behaviors (Generalized Reinforcer Value).

Ideally, bonding is bilateral and occurs at Level Three. It may, however, grow slowly through contact, be unilateral and progress.

William R. McCuller, Ph.D.[5]

---

or *resensitization*. To help a person make this journey from exclusion to inclusion, we must support him along the way with patience, understanding and imagination. We must start with what the person can tolerate, then help open his world, opportunity by opportunity.

[5] From conversations with Dr. William R. McCuller, Ph.D., circa June, 1995.

Connect
The previous chapter explored the three building blocks of Universal Enhancement–integration, participation and relationships. People who have been Outsiders for some time often lose the ties that bind them with people and places in their home communities. On many of the functional assessments of people coming out of institutional placements, we read such things as, "Does not bond with others," or "Avoids relationships." We now approach relationship building, or *connection*, as one of the tools of Universal Enhancement.

MAXIM: When you bond with people, they are less likely to behave in a way to disappoint you. ™

Connection is sometimes known in psychological circles as *reciprocal bonding*, a fancy name for "becoming friends." A psychologist with whom I worked has come up with an operant definition of bonding. Dr. McCuller's elegant description is another way of describing the process of developing a relationship.

Level One: What You Do to/for Me
Level One occurs when the person with whom you are bonding knows that you have access to something she wants. Even a cat, not renowned for its bonding abilities, can manage a relationship at this level. If you are the person with the can opener or the one who opens the front door, you are the cat's friend. There is a bond, but it is not personal. The neighbor who comes over to feed the cat when you are away will also be the object of the bond–if she has the can opener.

Many Level One relationships exist in institutional settings. In a relationship based on who has what and how I can get it (also called *politics*), Level One is about as far as a person can go. Thus, the nurse with the nasty-tasting medicine is avoided, and the man with the key to the dining room is a friend.

Some studies of the ways people in institutional settings form relationships indicate that many view all of their relationships as intimate.

Lacking experience with the range of closeness most of us have (from casual acquaintance to intimate lover), they are fooled into thinking that staff are their best friends.

Level Two: Relating to Familiar People

Level Two is a little more sophisticated. The bond is based not on the receipt of a specific reward but on a connection that has been made within a specific context. When I am out walking at the local park, there is a woman who always says hello and makes a friendly comment about the weather or about how good it is to be walking. I do not know her name or anything else about her. What we share is a common context–walking at the track. The nature of our bond is that I look forward to exchanging greetings with her when I see her.

This is the kind of bond we see in young children. We say, "She responds to familiar people." The message is, "I know you. You're supposed to be here. I feel comfortable when you are around."

Level Two bonding is quite common in institutional settings. In fact, a common developmental milestone is "Responds to familiar people." This type of bond develops through the process of paid staff appearing at time intervals (shifts), daily living events occurring as scheduled rou-

---

CONNECT

Nurture the establishment of friendships.
- Provide opportunity for interacting with individuals who are not paid to interact, not family members and who do not have disabilities.
- Recognize that developing a friendship takes time. Don't rush it.

Foster mutual smiles and touches.
- Demonstrate your connections with others through appropriate smiles and touches.

Promote a sense of humor.
- Have a good time: share laughter and the comic moments of life.

Celebrate special events, life's accomplishments and being together.

tines, and specific tasks being carried out by specific people. Those of us who have worked in settings that keep relationships on this level may have come to accept and even desire them. I feel good when a person to whom I offer supports and assistance recognizes me. But, how often are these relationships continued outside of the work setting? How many of us have "residents" sharing our Thanksgiving table unless it is our scheduled day to work?

Level Three: Having a Friend

Level Three is what we commonly describe as friendship. We like to be with a person in a wide variety of situations, and have come to know and care about her. The bond is bilateral; that is, the feeling is mutual. How does this development come about? Dr. McCuller suggests that it may grow slowly, from only one of the participants. Or, it may occur immediately, like falling in love. The hope is that bonding will occur, and the task is to help people who have had little experience of, or opportunity for, friendship to develop their capacity to form bonds.

Ralph Waldo Emerson wrote, "The only way to have a friend is to be one" (*Essays*: First Series [1841] Friendship).[6] How, then, is someone going to have a friend if he does not know how to be a friend? The answer is: He will have to learn. Being a friend involves knowing how to greet someone, respond to her overtures, and ask her to dinner. A friend also knows how to send flowers to a loved one in the hospital or a card to him on his birthday.

MAXIM: *Don't care for people; care about them.* ™

These are skills we all had to learn. Unfortunately, they are not often the kinds of skills that show up in the usual planning process for the people to whom we supply services and supports. In fact, we have sometimes been guilty of teaching staff to keep their distance in order to establish a therapeutic relationship.

[6] Ralph Waldo Emerson, *Friendship*, in *Selected Essays* (Chicago: Book Production Industries, Inc., 1959).

More creative and challenging than maintaining professional distance would be an admonition that each of us should model the skills of bonding. We need to give smiles and hugs, not just as reinforcers but as the building blocks of relationships. We need to be able to go up to someone who requires pervasive supports, give him a hug, and say, "I like you. You're a good guy," noncontingently, just because he is a good and valuable person.

Furthermore, we need to promote a sense of humor in the people to whom we provide supports. It's okay to laugh, tell a joke and share the comic moments of life. Humor breaks down barriers and builds up relationships. And, people with a sense of humor are more attractive than people who are dour and reserved.

Finally, we must celebrate life's special events together. Few activities do more to cement the bonding of relationships than the sharing of accomplishments and personal milestones. We can have a housewarming party (not an agency open house) to celebrate a person's new residence. We can have a party at a nearby pizza restaurant to celebrate a man's first paycheck. We can attend funerals, weddings and baby showers with the people we support. Participation in the activities of relating is the only way relationships can be formed.

Connections take time. We have to "fake it 'til we make it." We have to take what we can get closest to what we want. We have to work on mending, socialization and communication. And, we have to share our feelings and demonstrate caring. The result is worth the effort. Emerson added, later in his essay on friendship, "A friend may well be reckoned the masterpiece of Nature."[7]

Communicate

Another way of supporting a person in attaining the essence of a relationship is communication. Often, those of us who work with people who have limited communication skills are still stuck in the Developmental Model of communication. We want to communicate with a person on his level, so we talk with him in the simplistic way we would talk with a child, starting with simple words and only later, when we think he has made progress, expanding into sentences.

But, such limits on our communication also impose limits on our respect for him. We erect a barrier between him and Us when we are not willing to communicate the same way we would with our family and friends. We may find ourselves saying of a person who speaks no words, "She has no communication skills." Then, at the same planning meeting, we might discuss how to respond to her "tantrums" during which she rips her clothes and breaks furniture. Do we not realize that this "behavior" is a bold effort to communicate her needs? Maybe she is unhappy because a friend snubbed her at work today or her ear hurts because of an infection. Maybe she feels powerless to affect a rigid schedule. Maybe she just dislikes the color of the curtains or the style of the furniture!

MAXIM: *Anger communicates unmet needs. LISTEN!*

Simply stated, *anger communicates unmet needs. LISTEN!* Many of the challenging behaviors we see result from the frustration a per-

[7] Ralph Waldo Emerson, *Friendship*, in *Selected Essays* (Chicago: Book Production Industries, Inc., 1959).

> **"Violence is the language of the unheard."** -- Dr. Martin Luther King, Jr.

son with communication difficulties feels when no one listens to her. Exercising the skills of active listening, paying close attention, and not being too quick to say our own piece goes a long way toward accomplishing our goals of socialization and connection. Being able to communicate affect (how a person feels) is too often ignored when picture/symbol boards, manual signs, communication wallets, and voice synthesizers are used as supports in expressive communication. These devices and procedures may certainly help a person ask for more milk or tell us that he needs to use the bathroom. Being able to do these things does bring improvements in the person's quality of life, but how do we support being able to say, "I'm sad because my friend is away on vacation" or "I love you"?

MAXIM: *Violence is the language of the unheard.*
–Rev. Martin Luther King, Jr.

People learn how to express anger, sadness or happiness not by learning new words but by seeing others express their feelings. What if you lived in a place where no one ever laughed or told a joke, or the only tears you ever saw were tears of rage and pain? Share your feelings with the people you serve and support. Reciprocate when they smile.

You might be amazed at their responsiveness and how expressive they can be of their own feelings when they know someone will take the time and make the effort to listen.

TALE
Sharing Pete's Death

When I arrived for work at Charlie's home, he could see that there was something bothering me. I usually come in with a smile and ask Charlie about his day at the workshop. Today, I just didn't feel like doing that.

Charlie doesn't speak, but he came up to me and put his hand on my arm, looking into my face as if to ask, "What's wrong?" I tried to cover with a feeble smile, but a tear came out instead.

"I'm sorry, Charlie," I said. "I'm feeling kind of blue this afternoon. You see, this morning, I had to take my old dog, Pete, to the vet's and have him put to sleep."

MAXIM: *Share your feelings.*

Active Listening

Square off
Open
Leaning
Eye contact
Reflecting

My voice cracked as I related to Charlie the harrowing events of the morning–the difficult decision, followed by the actual death itself. I told about how I held my old friend in my arms. When I looked up from my narrative, there was a tear in Charlie's eye, too. Then, he tugged on my sleeve, his indication that he wanted me to go somewhere with him.

I followed Charlie into his bedroom where he began rummaging through a dresser drawer. Suddenly, he plucked an old, bent photo from the jumble of saved objects and junk that made up his "collections" drawer. He showed it to me. It was a photo of Charlie, squatting down to pet old Pete. It had been taken last summer at our picnic in the mountains.

I sat on Charlie's bed with him, and we both had a good cry. We will both miss Pete, but we will take comfort in the bond that has grown between us through sharing our common loss.

Initiate: to Cause to Begin

The word *initiate* has some marvelous dictionary definitions that contribute significantly to our understanding of the concept. The first definition is "to cause to begin." When we assist people who

---

COMMUNICATE

Exercise skills of listening.
- Role model listening to others.
- Listen slowly and carefully.

Share expressions of feelings.
- Share your feelings - show your emotional side.

Support self-determination and self-advocacy.
- Allow individuals to exercise control over their lives.
- Recognize that skills acquisition enhances self-determination.

require extensive support, particularly if they have spent a portion of their lives in places that manifest many institutional characteristics, the thing we are causing to begin is a life. Yes, a life. We are called upon to provide the opportunities and supports the person needs to build a meaningful life, filled with cherished persons, important rituals and significant events.

A person who is just now getting the opportunity to live among us cannot build a life around learning to apply underarm deodorant. *That's not where it's at.* It is not necessary to begin with childish skills in order to make a beginning. We must begin with the things that are important to the person who is receiving supports and services.

Initiate: to Introduce
The second dictionary meaning of *initiate* is "to introduce (a person) to a new field, interest, skill or activity." Our job is to introduce the person to choice making and relationship building, but also to stories about the activities she has actively participated in. We also get to assist her in telling others about skills she is proud of.

There is such a wonderful range of activities, attitudes and experiences that make up the quality of a life. We have the opportunity and honor to be the key that unlocks access to things a person may never have experienced before. What a shame it would be if we forfeited that opportunity because the person to whom we were providing support had yet to pass his "appropriate social greetings" program.

Introductions are an important part of our new role as community access workers, guides who help a person get past the Gatekeepers and barriers that are scattered through the community. When we are out and about (participating) with the person we are assisting, we must look for opportunities to introduce him to friends, neighbors, merchants and other business people.

When we walk into the greeting card shop with Edgar and see our friend Ethel, we can say, "Hi, Ethel. I'd like you to meet Edgar. He's new to the community, and I'm helping him find his way around."

MAXIM: *You do not have to prove yourself to have a reasonable life. –Todd Risley, Ph.D.*

INITIATE

- **Build upon the activities and items valued by the person– individualize.**
  - Identify strengths – they form the basis of future growth.

- **Promote rituals of membership.**
  - Encourage participation in activities that say "I belong."
  - Celebrate the milestones of developing a presence.

- **Introduce.**
  - Seize upon all opportunities to assist others in making new acquaintances.

- **Assure that the skills acquired enhance the quality of the person's life.**

Ethel might then turn from the card rack and say, "Pleased to meet you, Edgar," and shake his hand. Edgar may need a little prompting or assistance to follow through with the next step in this little conversational gambit, but that is our job.

Now that introductions have been made, we can engage in conversation with Ethel and learn that she is seeking a card for Walter, the grocery store manager. Tomorrow is Walter's birthday. Edgar now realizes that he knows Walter, too; Walter helped him a day earlier when he was weighing the potatoes. He, too, would like to get Walter a birthday card. He thanks Ethel for letting him know about Walter's birthday.

Pathway to Friendship

Every relationship/friendship one forms in his or her life, other than with family, is developed as a result of playing an active role (participating).

The relationships/friends one has nurtured as a(n)...

- Parishioner who collected the tithe at church
- Camper who won first place in diving at the Girl Scout or Boy Scout camp
- Employee who brought tomatoes to work from the garden
- Patient who consoled his roommate at the hospital
- Volunteer who raised funds for a worthy cause
- Neighbor who lent her garden tools
- Athlete who played shortstop on a softball team
- Student who played in the high school band
- Prisoner who served time following a conviction for income tax evasion
- Parent who volunteered time at his child's school as a room monitor
- Gambler who served as the "bank" in a weekly poker game

...enhance the quality of one's life. People who lack friends tend to lack roles.

Initiate: to Admit into Membership

The third definition of *initiate* gives us a glimpse into the mystery of what we have set about to do. It says that to initiate is "to admit into membership, as with ceremonies or ritual." This brings us back to Chapter 2, where habilitation was defined as imparting the skills one needed "to qualify."

People who have spent years living in some institutional setting and then enter our communities are like new immigrants to our country. They may not know the language, the customs, how to get around or how to do business. They have been excluded from membership in our society. They often have no network of supportive relationships and no points of access from which to develop a network.

Some appropriate initiatory activities are:

- Obtaining a state-issued photo ID card from the driver's license bureau (even if the person does not have the skills to drive), thus becoming a "card carrying" member of the community

- Registering to vote, thus being "on the list" of people who count

- Getting a job, whether paid or volunteer, thus becoming someone who "makes a contribution"

- Joining a Neighborhood Watch organization, thus becoming a person who cares about his neighbors.

MAXIM: It's not attention people are seeking; it's prestige. ™

We must be creative in helping people find ways of belonging. With Universal Enhancement, everyone, every human being on this planet, is already, right now, qualified to be a full, participating member of the human race, with all the rights and privileges that entails. If one of our fellow humans has not been admitted to membership because he does not qualify, it is our task to design and initiate the appropriate ceremonies or rituals to say, "Welcome. You're one of us."

TOOLBOX
Universal Enhancement Checklist

This checklist can help you assess the extent to which the important processes of Universal Enhancement are occurring in any setting. Give each item a score from 0 to 10. A zero indicates the complete absence of the condition. A score of five means the glass is half full. A ten is full realization of that process.

Mend

• Are obstacles in the person's life identified?	
• Does the environment include modifications to hurdle those obstacles?	
• Do all staff participate in designing creative Life Stiles to support each person in overcoming barriers to a full life?	
• Is gentle physical support used to redirect challenging behaviors and protect from injury?	
• Is choice-making supported as an option to challenging behavior?	
• Are temporary medication plans based on adequate assessment and regular review?	
• Are new medication doses started low and increased slowly as the need arises?	
SUBTOTAL	

Socialize

• Is tolerance of others modeled and encouraged?	
• Are staff teaching kindness and caring through role modeling?	
• Are people interacting with others in a way that is not task-focused?	
• Are people allowed to declare their own personal space?	

• Is attention and praise provided for everyone's interests and gifts?	
• Are occasions provided for successful interaction?	
• Are people encouraged to give and do for others?	
• Are expressions of appreciation promoted?	
SUBTOTAL	

Connect

• Is the establishment of friendships nurtured?	
• Are opportunities provided for interacting with individuals who are not paid to interact?	
• Do staff recognize that friendship takes time and should not be rushed?	
• Are connections with others modeled through appropriate smiles and touches?	
• Is a sense of humor promoted?	
• Are good times shared?	
• Are celebrations included such as special events?	
SUBTOTAL	

Communicate

• Do staff understand and exercise the skills of listening?	
• Is listening to others modeled and reinforced?	
• Do staff listen slowly and carefully?	
• Do people share expressions of feeling?	
• Do staff model the sharing of feeling and revealing their emotional sides?	
• Is self-determination and self-advocacy supported in observable ways?	
• Are people encouraged to exercise control over their own lives?	

• Can staff point to ways they demonstrate how skill acquisition enhances self-determination?	
SUBTOTAL	

Initiate

• Are staff aware of individual preferences?	
• Are individual strengths (as well as deficits) identified?	
• Do new staff and new residents participate in rituals of membership?	
• Does everyone have the opportunity to participate in activities that say, *I belong*?	
• Are the milestones of developing a Presence–such as achievements, new memberships, and new relationships–celebrated?	
• Do staff look for opportunities to make introductions?	
• Is the formation of relationships that can become natural supports encouraged and achieved?	
SUBTOTAL	
GRAND TOTAL	

Scores (perfect = 380)

0-150   Is this an institution?
151-250   Some old paradigms are still at work here.
251-300   There's a new day dawning!
301-380   Universal Enhancement is making everyone's life better. Celebrate!

12

Having a Life...and Beyond

It is with some hesitation and a good deal of humility that I propose another approach to supporting persons with disabilities and other Outsiders. I have experienced and been affected by many changes during my years of working to provide needed supports and services to all kinds of people whose conditions or circumstances have caused them to be cast aside.

I have seen, and even been a part of, ways of behaving toward Outsiders that excluded, demeaned and dehumanized. I have met each new guiding philosophy for the services we deliver with the joy and exhilaration that come from discovering a better way of doing a job I care very much about. I have worked under the Medical/Custodial Model; I was a caretaker beholden to doctors and nurses for the ways I perceived and related to patients.

I was excited about the possibilities of the Developmental Model, and I strove mightily to help people move up on those developmental data document graphs. I saw incredible change driven by the principles of the Habilitation Model, as the ICF-MR regulations drove agencies to some semblance of normalization.

I advocated and propagated each new approach. But, I was always willing to leave each adopted philosophy behind, eager to move forward and embrace a better way.

I have never before been as enthusiastic about the promises held out for a new way of looking at our work as I am at the prospects of

Universal Enhancement. I see it as a way of keeping the excitement in our work. I teach, coach, and consult the content and principles of Universal Enhancement daily, and I am frequently asked how I maintain my enthusiasm. Those who are not yet believers and the uninitiated will soon learn that Universal Enhancement inspires those who embrace it and motivates them to achieve the vision. It is exciting. It brings great energy, an enthusiasm that lights the way through years of hard work, to those of us who work in the field of human services.

But is Universal Enhancement just another step along this long and sometimes tedious road? Will I be back in a few years, discussing and writing about how I used to believe in Universal Enhancement, but now I have gone beyond that to...whatever? It is possible. I hope I will be open enough to new thinking to see and accept another, better way when we find it or it finds us.

Meanwhile, Universal Enhancement offers innovations the other models do not. In fact, it is not really a model at all; nor is it some kind of static belief, a school of thought that has dogmas and creeds that must be observed. It is, rather, an ongoing process that changes all the time; it is synergistic, organic and holistic. It applies the same kinds of ever-changing, inconsistent, growth-producing principles to the lives of Outsiders that most of us take for granted in our own lives.

Universal Enhancement is not a template or standard that can be used to judge whether or not people have reached some imagined goal. It allows for failures as well as successes; solitude as well as intimacy; dejection as well as elation.

There is no downside to Universal Enhancement. It is not a new technology born in the halls of academia that must be tested or proven. It is not some fantasy of social engineering, a give-away program that will bankrupt the nation. It violates no standards or regulations. It poses no ethical dilemmas or harmful side effects. There is, quite simply, no reason not to follow the course of Universal Enhancement.

Why Should It Be Any Different?

The two principal differences between Universal Enhancement and all earlier models of service are that Universal Enhancement: 1) provides assurances that the person who needs support and assistance is the one who makes the decisions about how, where, and by whom those supports and assistance are provided; and 2) removes the social barriers that segregate people who have been treated as Outsiders as a result of their disabilities or other personal characteristics. These differences are the essence of the critical paradigm shift that is sweeping the field of human services.

If you have viewed people who are different from Normatives as "them," as people who need some kind of life that is radically different from the life you want, Universal Enhancement requires nothing short of a conversion experience. In the same way that a person can be struck by a spiritual awakening, the focus of Universal Enhancement makes the world appear a different place. Once you see it, it is so obvious that you wonder how you could have missed it. The shift is like those 3-D pictures that look, at first, like nothing but splotches of color. Once the image comes into focus, you have difficulty not seeing it.

One of the working titles for this book was "Why Should It Be Any Different?" Asking that question helps us see that the essence of Universal Enhancement is that we stop thinking of people who are over sixty-five years old, or have mental illness, physical disabilities or intellectual disabilities as being essentially different from us. Instead of asking, "What do they want?" or "What do they need?" we begin to ask, "What does Harriet want?" or "What does Raymond need?"

But, of whom do we ask those questions? We ask Harriet and Raymond. This is the final step, the piece that breaks down the differences. We can no longer afford the luxury of believing that just because we are professionals, family members or authorities of some kind, we know better than Harriet or Raymond what they want and need out of life.

Equally important is that we begin to empathize with people who are Outsiders. No longer seeing them as wholly alien, we can ask,

"What would I want if I were in their shoes?" That is the standard we must use. We can no longer be experts doing to or caretakers doing for. We must see ourselves as supports, working side by side with the people to whom we provide support, even staying in the background when necessary, for that is probably how we would like to be treated, were our status exchanged for theirs. We must *do with*.

> **MAXIM:** *Do not treat others the way you would wish to be treated; but rather treat others the way you would treat yourself under the most challenging of circumstances.*

Relationships

We emphasize relationships, not only for the sake of the person who needs supports but also, and perhaps more importantly, for our own sake. For it is relationship that makes everyone's life more worthwhile.

According to Karl Menninger, "The establishment or re-establishment of relationship with fellow human beings is the basic architecture of normal life... To live, we say, is to love, and vice versa."[8]

If *relationship* does, indeed, form the basic architecture of normal life, then that is where we need to build. We must leave our training structures behind and harken to the structures of the human heart and spirit.

Fulfillment of the Promise

Universal Enhancement is for everybody. That is what makes it universal. Universal Enhancement will be realized when we no longer define a quality life in terms of treatment teams, program plans, schedules and menus. When we seek to remove the barriers that cause handicaps and stop segregating people on the basis of their abilities, Universal Enhancement will become a reality.

The fulfillment of the promise of Universal Enhancement does not depend on the professional community adopting new assess-

---

[8] Karl Menninger, *The Vital Balance: The Life Process in Mental Illness* (New York: Viking Press, 1963), 294.

ment devices or training techniques. Rather, and most importantly, it requires the efforts of good men and women everywhere who will see people as people and treat them as neighbors. Indeed, we can be–should be–midwives who are only helping during the transition from the old ways to the new.

Universal Enhancement will have happened when we who work as professionals in the field of services to Outsiders will be out of a job,

when families, friends, coworkers, choir members and grocery store employees will give support and assistance to everyone who needs it. Universal Enhancement will come to fruition when everyone, regardless of how they look, how smart they are or how many things they have difficulty doing, will be treated with dignity and respect and appreciation by all.

About the Author

Thomas E. Pomeranz, Ed.D., is an authority, trainer, clinician and consultant in the field of services for people with disabilities. He serves as President and CEO of Universal LifeStiles, based in Indianapolis, Indiana. And, he is the creator of Universal Enhancement, which teaches strategies that promote community participation and support people to lead meaningful lives.

Tom is a Policy Fellow and Visiting Lecturer for Minot State University – North Dakota Center for Persons with Disabilities, a University Center of Excellence.

Over the last forty years, Tom has conducted thousands of seminars and programs throughout the United States and Canada. He was the keynote speaker at the Fifth International Conference on Developmental Disabilities and Aging in Cyprus.

He has held a variety of top-level, administrative posts in community-based service organizations and at three large, state-operated facilities. Tom received his bachelor's and master of science degrees in special education and a doctorate in mental health administration from Indiana University, followed by post-graduate work with the University of Notre Dame in the area of experimental psychology.

CPSIA information can be obtained at www.ICGtesting.com
Printed in the USA
LVOW051924250812

295933LV00001B/8/P